WITHDRAWN

HARVARD LIBRARY

WITHDRAWN

BASTILLE WITNESS

The Prison Autobiography of Madame Guyon (1648–1717)

Introduction and notes by Nancy Carol James

Translation and notes by Sharon D. Voros

University Press of America,® Inc.
Lanham · Boulder · New York · Toronto · Plymouth, UK

Copyright © 2012 by
University Press of America,® Inc.
4501 Forbes Boulevard
Suite 200
Lanham, Maryland 20706
UPA Acquisitions Department (301) 459-3366

Estover Road
Plymouth PL6 7PY
United Kingdom

All rights reserved
Printed in the United States of America
British Library Cataloging in Publication Information Available

Library of Congress Control Number: 2011940401
ISBN: 978-0-7618-5772-3 (clothbound : alk. paper)
eISBN: 978-0-7618-5773-0

A translation of RÉCITS DE CAPTIVITÉ written by
Madame Jeanne de la Mothe Guyon,
Ed. Marie-Louise Gondal, Grenoble: Éditions Jérôme Millon, 1992.

∞™ The paper used in this publication meets the minimum requirements of American National Standard for Information Sciences—Permanence of Paper for Printed Library Materials, ANSI Z39.48-1992

For my husband Chip Voros and

for my sons John and Ulric Dahlgren.

Sharon D. Voros

For my mother, Eve Keene James.

Nancy Carol James

Table of Contents

Acknowledgements	vii
Introduction	ix
Translator's Notes	xxvii
Chapter One. Arrest and Imprisonment in Vincennes	1
Chapter Two. Behind Closed Doors in Vaugirard	20
Chapter Three. New Trials in Vaugirard	32
Chapter Four. The Letter from the Priest of Saint-Sulpice	45
Chapter Five. The Letter from Father La Combe	58
Chapter Six. In the Bastille: In the Shadow of a Trial	69
Chapter Seven. In the Bastille: The Final Battle	83
Epilogue	98
Bibliography	102
Index	108

Acknowledgements

First of all, I would especially like to express my appreciation and gratitude to Dr. Nancy C. James for inviting me to translate Madame Guyon's prison memoirs, based on the text established by the French scholar Marie-Louise Gondal. Special thanks also to the editor at Éditions Jérôme in Grenoble, Marie-Claude Carrara, who graciously put me in contact with Madame Gondal, whom I was able to meet in Lyon in 2009. Thanks to them, we have the authorization to use this edition as the basis for this translation. Also, I would especially like to express my gratitude to Madame Gondal for tracking down the manuscript that she had found in the Jesuit library, Bibliothèque des Fontaines in Chantilly, now closed. She took me to the Bibliothèque Part-Dieu where many early editions of Madame Guyon's publications are now housed. Later in Paris, I was able to consult the manuscript available at the Jesuit Centre Sèvres. I would like to present my thanks to Audrey Gaquin, Professor of French, and Sylvain Guarda, Professor of French and Chair, and Heidi Rey, Department Secretary, of the Languages and Cultures Department, United States Naval Academy for their unfailing support for research, and to the Naval Academy Research Council for the grant I received at the beginning of this project. I would like to thank Renato Barahona, Professor of History at the University of Illinois, Chicago, for reading the draft and providing valuable suggestions. I am also especially grateful to Pierre and Evelyne Ghertman for their suggestions and encouragement when I was on sabbatical in Paris. They put me in contact with their niece, the French historian Michèle Fogel, who lent me books on seventeenth- French spirituality. Finally, I would like to express my deepest gratitude, love, and appreciation to my family, my husband Charles D. Voros, my sons John and Ulric Dahlgren, my daughters-in-law Jessica and Nasrin, and my granddaughter Nadia, who have always provided support, good humor, and encouragement.

Sharon D. Voros, Ph.D.
Professor of Spanish and French
United States Naval Academy

I thank Dr. Sharon Voros for her professional help and excellent translation of *Bastille Witness*. Her understanding of Madame Guyon is superlative and I appreciate her help with this book. I want to thank Dr. Carlos Eire of Yale University for his help with the scholarship surrounding Madame Guyon.

I appreciate the help of Carol Armbruster, the Italian and French specialist at the Library of Congress, who helped me locate my first edition of this important manuscript. The Rev. Dr. Hugh Brown and the Rev. Dr. Elly Sparks Brown have provided important theological discussions during the creation of this book.

I want to thank my family, Roger, Hannah, and Melora for their help and love during the writing of this book.

The Rev. Nancy Carol James, Ph.D.
St. John's, Lafayette Square
Washington, D.C.

The picture of Madame Guyon on the cover is by an unknown artist. The drawing originally appeared in *Little Journeys to the Homes of the Great* by Elbert Hubbard published by The Roycrofters in 1916.

Introduction

Born in Montargis, France, in 1648, Jeanne Marie Bouvier de La Mothe Guyon showed her interest in religious experience as a young child.[1] Madame Guyon's aristocratic family was well connected to King Louis' court at Versailles. Both of Jeanne's parents had been previously married and their large, blended family experienced frequent conflicts. Because of their busy family life, Madame Guyon had little formal education except being educated by the Ursuline sisters in 1655. At a young age she frequently spent time alone reading through the Bible and the writings of the saints, such as Francis de Sales and Jane de Chantal. She became devoted to her Catholic religion and developed a reputation for eloquence in public conversation. Out of her personal devotion grew a desire to become a nun, a goal that her parents denied.

When Jeanne was fifteen years of age, her father arranged a marriage for her with a wealthy thirty-eight year old man, Monsieur Jacques Guyon, Lord of Chesnoy and of Champoulet. From the start this marriage was a mismatch with Madame Guyon readily expressing her ideas and her husband attempting to change her personality. Jeanne's husband and mother-in-law started a program of actively controlling and disciplining her that led to an extremely unhappy home environment. She was allowed only limited social interaction and perfunctory participation in her religion.

At the age of nineteen Madame Guyon sought guidance about her spiritual frustration from a Franciscan monk, Abbé Archange Enguerrand.[2] The monk answered, "It is, Madame, because you seek outside what you have within. Accustom yourself to seek God in your heart, and you will find him there." Madame Guyon described the experience of this insight like an arrow going through her heart. She stated that the interior sweetness of God caused her to find a new happiness.

Following this, Madame Guyon claimed a freedom based on the experience of God within.[3] Her spirituality shaped every area of her life. On July 22, 1672, in an experience of prayer, Guyon committed herself to Jesus and vowed to "take for my spouse our Lord" and "to give myself to him for spouse, though unworthy."[4] She honored this personal commitment the rest of her life.

Madame Guyon took an active role in raising her own children and refused to leave them when they developed smallpox. Madame Guyon grieved after two of her children died, even as she recovered from her own case of smallpox that left her scarred and weakened. Despite her efforts, Guyon knew a troubled relationship with her eldest son and regretted their loss of rapport due to the family conflicts. Guyon took care of her husband during his many illnesses that eventually led to his death in 1676.

As a young and wealthy widow, Madame Guyon handled her own finances and placed much of the money in trusts for her children. She began spiritual direction with a Barnabite priest named Abbé François La Combe and sought increased opportunities for her own spiritual development.[5] In 1681 Madame Guyon decided to move near Geneva to develop her ministry close to where her spiritual director Abbé La Combe lived. Together Madame Guyon and Abbé La Combe started hospitals and worked as spiritual directors for any who desired help. Both the rich and poor sought their assistance.

The Bishop of Geneva, Jean D'Aranthon, requested that Madame Guyon contribute some of her wealth to his projects. She explained that the money was placed in trust for her children and declined his request. In an attempt then to gain control over her, the bishop devised a plan for her to become a mother superior of the religious order called the *Nouvelles Catholiques*.[6] Guyon declined the bishop's plan. After this, rumors developed about Guyon and La Combe's relationship; Guyon wrote, "They circulated a story that I was running about with him . . . and a hundred malicious absurdities."[7]

Madame Guyon also writes in her *Autobiography* about a problem in the Geneva diocese. A nun sought Madame Guyon's assistance after a highly placed diocesan official known as the "Little Bishop" sexually harassed her. Madame Guyon discussed this situation with Bishop Jean D'Aranthon. Following her intervention with this problem, Bishop D'Aranthon expelled both Madame Guyon and Abbé La Combe from this diocese.

Madame Guyon and Abbé La Combe found new opportunities for ministry in other places in Europe. They received criticism about their relationship, although both protested that La Combe was the spiritual director for Madame Guyon. The places to which Madame Guyon traveled included towns throughout Switzerland, Italy and France. During these travels from 1681-1685, Madame Guyon wrote many of her famous books, including *A Short and Easy Method of Prayer, Spiritual Torrents*, and her Biblical commentaries.

Madame Guyon's book *A Short and Easy Method of Prayer* became popular after a counselor of the Parliament at Grenoble published this book. After many read this book, Madame Guyon's reputation for spiritual wisdom began to spread. Both lay and ordained sought her out for private counsel. Yet Madame Guyon's growing public ministry drew attention to and increased the controversy for both her and Abbé La Combe.

Guyon continued her ministry even after receiving warnings from authorities about her controversial work. Guyon wrote that some monks were "vexed that a woman...should be so sought after."[8] Some called her a diabolical witch and sorceress. Yet Guyon believed that the predominant influence in her life was her intense love of God. In her *Autobiography* she writes, "I loved Him and I burnt with love, because I loved Him. I loved Him in such a way that I could only love Him; but in loving Him I had no motive but himself."[9]

Madame Guyon's half-brother Abbé de La Mothe was also Abbé La Combe's superior in the Barnabite order. La Mothe accused his sister and La Combe of moral improprieties and wrote many church officials complaining about La Combe's alleged scandalous behavior with Guyon. He also accused La Combe of Quietism by showing church officials propositions of Molinos and stating that they were the errors of Abbé La Combe.[10] Despite the absence of a legal right to benefit from the Guyon money, La Mothe criticized Guyon's handling of her own finances. La Mothe requested that both Madame Guyon and Abbé La Combe return to Paris. Despite Guyon's warnings about the hidden intentions of her half-brother, La Combe returned to Paris only to find that he was accused of heresy and the subject of an Inquisition.

The French Roman Catholic Church charged Abbé La Combe with the heresy of Quietism, creating a threatening and ominous situation for him, Madame Guyon and their supporters: lengthy incarceration or death by burning at the stake was now likely. After quick proceedings, La Combe was found guilty of heresy and began his life-long incarceration. He suffered twenty-seven years of incarceration before his death in 1715. Once the Inquisition had successfully destroyed Abbé La Combe's life and career, they turned their dreaded powers against Madame Guyon. This action caused fear among many of the French royalty who were regarded as her friends.

Madame Guyon could now expect the same treatment as Abbé La Combe. On January 29, 1688, Guyon received a *lettre de cachet* from Louis XIV.[11] This letter with the royal seal ordered her imprisonment and deprived her of the right to appeal. Guyon was incarcerated at the Visitation Convent in an unventilated room and was kept under constant surveillance. A church official frequently interrogated her. Guyon argued that she was being held to the standards of a highly-educated theologian, although she was a self-educated lay woman.

Guyon's friends and relatives began a strong advocacy for her release from incarceration. An order for Guyon's release came in September 1688, because her cousin, Madame de La Maisonfort, discussed the situation with Madame de Maintenon, the secret wife of Louis XIV. Madame de Maintenon arranged for Madame Guyon's release from this eight month long incarceration.

Even after this incarceration, Madame Guyon continued her writing and spiritual counseling. Shortly after her release, she met Abbé François de Salignac de la Mothe-Fénelon at a social gathering near Versailles. They developed a close friendship based on their shared spiritual beliefs. The historian Duc de Saint-Simon writes about Fénelon and Guyon saying that their "sublimes amalgamated."[12] Saint-Simon emphasized Guyon's love of solitude saying that she was "as a woman all in God, whose humility and whose love of contemplation and solitude kept her within the strictest limits, and whose fear, above all, was that she should become known."[13]

Abbé Fénelon's career was rising and in 1689 he became the tutor for Louis XIV's grandson, the Duc de Bourgogne. This gave Fénelon a powerful position in the court of Louis XIV. Madame Guyon joined with Fénelon, Madame de Maintenon and others in a position of leadership to meet regularly to pray for the leadership of France and for a spiritual renewal at the court at Versailles. This group was called the Court Cenacle or Convent of the Court. In 1696 Abbé Fénelon also became the archbishop of Cambray after his consecration by Jacques Bossuet, Bishop of Meaux, in the chapel at Saint-Cyr.

Madame de Maintenon invited Madame Guyon to teach her method of prayer at the school at Saint-Cyr for the daughters of the war-ruined, impoverished nobility. Guyon's theology from *A Short and Easy Method of Prayer* spread throughout the school and influenced the adolescent students and their teachers. Some clerics who came to Saint-Cyr became concerned about Guyon's theology and her spiritual direction, calling them Quietist. The bishop of Chartres and Saint-Cyr, Paul Godet, told Madame de Maintenon that Guyon was harming the order of the school by her teaching. On May 2, 1693, Madame de Maintenon issued a command that Madame Guyon could not visit Saint-Cyr again. Guyon submitted to this order.

Madame de Maintenon began to advocate for the second incarceration of Madame Guyon and hoped that Archbishop Fénelon would join in this request. Instead, Fénelon publicly stated that the writings of Madame Guyon belonged in the accepted mystic tradition of the Roman Catholic Church and, as such, were not heretical.

At this point the crucial decision was made by Guyon and Fénelon to invite the intervention of Bishop Bossuet into the situation. They believed that he would save Guyon from another incarceration. Bossuet, though, read Madame Guyon's prolific writings and did not approve of them. Bishop Bossuet and Archbishop Fénelon began a long public debate about the theology of Madame Guyon. A group of bishops decided to have a series of conferences that would decide the question of the orthodoxy of Madame Guyon. Many understood that ultimately it was the very essence of Christian spirituality that was at issue here.

This committee met at Issy, a rural area south of Paris. Along with the two other participants, Abbé Louis Tronson (a former teacher of Fénelon), and Louis-Antoine de Noailles, the Bishop of Chalons, they convened from July 1694, until March 1695 to analyze carefully the theology of Madame Guyon. Their meetings became known as the Issy Conferences. This group made its existence confidential so that Archbishop François de Harlay of Paris would not have to be invited to join the group, since Harlay was neither respected as a theologian nor as a person of integrity.

Archbishop Harlay became angered when he learned of these secret meetings occurring in his diocese in which he had not been invited to participate. He requested a meeting with Guyon. Following the advice of Bossuet, however, Guyon refused to meet with Harlay. Consequently, Harlay officially censured Guyon's books by placing them on the Catholic Index of Prohibited Books, a form of book condemnation originating in the Counter-Reformation.

Introduction xiii

During the Issy Conferences Bossuet and Fénelon struggled over a possible condemnation of Guyon, with both of them retreating from their acknowledged perspectives on her theology. In 1695 all of the participants signed the Thirty-Four Articles produced by them about mysticism and the controversy surrounding Quietism. Written in the form of a catechism of the church, this document also issued a list of condemned books that were judged to contain the Quietism heresy. Guyon was not condemned in these Issy Articles.

The Thirty-Four Articles of the Issy conference were published and widely circulated in 1695, after being signed by all participants in this lengthy series of meetings. Throughout these articles runs the theme of allowing freedom for all believers in their different modes of religious expressions, although these expressions are subject to the judgment of the episcopacy. For a "small number of chosen ones," though, this group stated that they "leave them to the judgment of the Almighty," acknowledging that in Job is given an example of an unusual religious experience not understood by many.[14] All of the acts of virtues, along with certain liturgical offerings such as the Lord's Prayer and the Apostle's Creed, were affirmed as Christian obligations, with the proviso that all these acts are united in love. The participants in the Issy Conference united behind these articles, with both Bishop Bossuet and Archbishop Fénelon signing them. Following this Madame Guyon assented to this peaceful agreement. "He (Bishop Bossuet) brought me the articles composed at Issi. I asked him the explanation of some passages, and I signed them."[15] The controversy should have been settled at this point, with the pacific unity that reigned in these Thirty-Four Articles.

Madame Guyon then went to live in Bossuet's cathedral town of Meaux in the Daughters of St. Mary convent in January 1695, seeking Bossuet's protection from Archbishop Harlay of Paris. Contrary to her expectations, Bossuet accused Guyon of heresy. Fénelon started rising to Jeanne's defense, even speaking to King Louis XIV about this situation. Finally Guyon asked Bossuet for permission to leave the convent to which he agreed. Later Bossuet stated that Guyon had left against his will. Guyon writes,

> Hardly had I arrived when the Bishop of Meaux repented having let me go out of his diocese. What made him change . . . is that when giving an account to Madame de Maintenon of the terms in which this affair was concluded, she let him know she was dissatisfied with the attestation he had given me.[16]

Bishop Bossuet took the lead in requesting the condemnation of Madame Guyon. One follower of Guyon believed that he did so because Louis' wife, Madame de Maintenon, desired this goal. The author of the *Supplement to the Life of Madame Guyon* states that Bossuet's imprisonment orders for Guyon were so bold that even an "audacious minister would not have countersigned them without fear."[17] The author wrote about Bossuet, saying that the "promise that was given to him in case of a condemnation was the archbishopric of Paris and the hat of a cardinal."[18] Bossuet publicly attacked both his former protégé Fénelon and Madame Guyon.

Bossuet argued the case that Madame Guyon was a dangerous criminal who needed to be incarcerated. After news of her possible second arrest, Guyon's friends encouraged her to leave France in order to save herself. Guyon refused that option. Instead, she hid herself under an assumed name in Paris from July 9, 1695, until her arrest on December 27, 1695, when a French policeman named Desgrez discovered her hiding place. After her arrest, the French state authorities decided to incarcerate her along with her two maids in the dungeon at the Vincennes.

Madame Guyon continually requested that her case be turned over to the secular authorities rather than tried by church officials because she expected higher standards of justice from the government officials. Bishop Bossuet and other church officials denied all of her requests to be placed solely under secular authorities.

The Lieutenant-General of the Police Gabriel Nicolas de La Reynie first interrogated Madame Guyon at length while she was imprisoned at Vincennes. Guyon had no legal counsel and developed her specific way of enduring the interrogations based on a scripture that encouraged no forethought. This scripture counsels the believer to trust the direction of the Holy Spirit given in that same hour. "And when they bring you to trial and deliver you up, do not be anxious beforehand what you are to say; but say whatever is given you in that hour, for it is not you who speak but the Holy Spirit."(Mark 13:9-11) Guyon believed that the Holy Spirit inspired her answers during these interrogations and described an experience of peace during her incarceration that exemplifies her theology. She writes, "The central depth of my heart was full of that joy which you give to those who love you, in the midst of the greatest crosses."[19]

During one interrogation, she was asked to write a letter declaring that Abbé La Combe was a dangerous heretic. She refused. After threats about her continued resistance, Guyon stated,

> Sir, although I suffer here all that one can suffer because of the continual pain that has overwhelmed me for such a long time along with the harsh treatment they do to make me suffer, I declare to you that I prefer to stay here all my life than to be set free by such a means. Nothing in the world is capable of breaking me.[20]

One time Guyon committed what she called an infidelity when she planned her responses ahead of time. On this occasion, Guyon believed that she created troubles for herself by not answering the questions well. She regretted her unfaithfulness.

After the series of long interrogations, La Reynie declared Madame Guyon innocent of the charges and told her she would be released. Yet the church authorities ignored La Reynie's judgment and arranged for her transfer to other incarcerations. On October 16, 1696, Guyon was transferred to a convent at

Introduction

Vaugirard. On June 4, 1698, French authorities transported Madame Guyon to her incarceration in the Bastille.[21]

Along with pursuing the condemnation of Fénelon, the French authorities aggressively sought to prove Guyon's guilt as a dangerous heretic. The author of *Supplement to the Life of Madame Guyon* states that there were "searches in all the places where she had been since her youth, examinations happened in the provinces, both far and near, of all the persons that she had known." The authorities conducting these interrogations of her acquaintances used "threats, promises and prisons to make them speak against her."[22]

In 1697 at the height of the Great Conflict, Fénelon published a book advocating for mysticism called *The Maxims of the Saints* in which he indirectly defends Guyon's theology. King Louis XIV, Bishop Bossuet and Archbishop Fénelon all requested that Pope Innocent XII rule on the orthodoxy of *Maxims of the Saints*.

Bishop Bossuet responded to Fénelon's *Maxims of the Saints* with his book titled *Quakerism á-la-mode, or A History of Quietisme: Particularly that of the Lord Arch-bishop of Cambray and Madame Guyone*. In his book Bossuet creates negative images of Madame Guyon while ridiculing her thought. When describing Guyon's prayer of silence, Bossuet says ironically that Guyon is like a "Nurse that bursts out with Milk,"[23] and creates an image of a nude Guyon by repeatedly saying that her over-flowing grace causes "the bursting of her Cloaths [sic] in two places by that frightful plentitude."[24] Throughout Bossuet's book *Quakerism á-la-Mode*, references are made to the possibility of Guyon being burned at the stake for her beliefs. Bossuet considered this a conceivable punishment for the heresy of Quietism in France. The frequency with which this image of burning at the stake, referred to as Guyon going to "the fire" or to be "burnt,"[25] creates this likelihood of capital punishment as a feasible choice after her expected condemnation.

During this time, Archbishop Fénelon steadfastly refused to align himself with those accusing Madame Guyon of heresy.[26] Because of this, Louis XIV stripped Fénelon of his position as royal tutor. On August 3, 1697, Louis banished Fénelon from Versailles. To the end of his days, Fénelon defended the orthodoxy of Madame Guyon's books.

In 1699 after careful deliberation by a committee of cardinals, Pope Innocent XII responded to the *Maxims of the Saints* by issuing a papal brief censuring twenty-three propositions of this book. This papal brief was considered a light criticism, because the Pope did not choose the form of papal bull, a much stronger form of condemnation. Fénelon was prohibited from spreading what the church thought to be incorrect beliefs. Pope Innocent XII wrote in his brief, "Damnatio & prohibitio libri . . . cui titulus, *Explication des Maximes des Saints sur la vie Interieure*."[27] The main thrust of the document is that Fénelon overemphasized the passivity of the believer in seeking eternal salvation, rather than the active search for salvation. Fénelon's belief that assurance of salvation was derived from the virtue of hope rather than love was also condemned.

Nothing was found to convict Guyon of both the secular and ecclesiastical charges. In 1700 Bishop Bossuet called for a reunion of the bishops from the conference at Issy. At this meeting the bishops declared Madame Guyon innocent of all moral charges and stated that she had done nothing wrong. Three years later on March 24, 1703, Madame Guyon was released from the Bastille. Because of her poor health, she was carried out of the Bastille on a litter. Guyon stated that she had forgiven those who had unjustly persecuted and incarcerated her. In Guyon's theology one is to have compassion for those who sin because of the serious ramifications of their behavior both in this life and in eternity.

Initially Madame Guyon was released to the legal custody of her eldest son. Their conflicts that had begun in childhood continued. Authorities then granted freedom to Madame Guyon who found a small house near her youngest daughter. According to *Supplement to the Life of Madame Guyon*, she was actually in exile in her own homeland, living close to her daughter's home in Blois the last fourteen years of her life. She corresponded with people around the world, including with her colleague Archbishop Fénelon. In one letter to Fénelon, Guyon addressed the issue of their disappointed hopes for a purified church. Guyon states, "In respect of the time that these things will happen, these words have been impressed on me. We are not granted the knowledge of the time and the moment that God will reserve for his power."[28]

The Great Conflict had raised much curiosity about Guyon's books. Many of her books, especially her *Autobiography, A Short and Easy Method of Prayer*, and commentary on the *Song of Songs*, were well received throughout Europe and the New World. Madame Guyon welcomed many visitors from around the world in her home. In particular, English and Scottish Protestants came to see Guyon and sometimes traveled on to talk with Archbishop Fénelon at Cambray. The Scotch author Chevalier André-Michel de Ramsay wrote that she visited with the English as if they were her spiritual children. Frequently the Protestants assembled in her apartment, which was illegal and made places to hide in the curtains around her bed in case the authorities raided her apartment. These Protestant followers largely sought her wisdom about her personal relationship with the Holy Spirit.

In Guyon's theology of the Holy Spirit her central or principal questions were, who is the Holy Spirit and how does the Holy Spirit act in human lives? She defines the Holy Spirit as "Love of the Father and of the Son, and thus the love with which God loves men; and He is the union of the Divine Persons, so He is the link that binds pure souls to Christ."[29] Another definition of the Holy Spirit is "this Spirit (which is, which was, and which will be, the will and love of God communicated to men.)"[30]

Guyon called this love between God and humanity pure love which is an unmediated power. This love overflowed from God to human beings who return this to God. Prayer is the medium for pure love. Through prayer the believer opened an interior spiritual world that conveyed pure love to others. The fulfillment caused by pure love led the person to allow openly more of the actions of the Holy Spirit. Guyon concluded that individual believers should give up a life of propriety and of self-interest, in order to allow the "crucifying operations of the divine spirit" to intervene.[31]

Guyon wrote frequently about these crucifying operations known in the testing of God. In a spiritual test, the person finds opposition from powerful forces. During this time, the person needs to find interior strength and claim spiritual gifts not otherwise known. Guyon stated that these spiritual tests witness to the person's purity of faith. She described Job's innocent suffering and Jesus' temptations in the wilderness as examples of testing sent from God. During tests that cause suffering, the believer becomes united to God and hence the believer enjoys the resources and strength of God. When suffering ceased in her own life, Guyon prayed for more suffering. Guyon understood her incarceration in the Bastille as a test from God and attempted to meet this challenge with interior faith.

Guyon stated that the believer must abandon or surrender his or her life to God in order to allow this work of the Holy Spirit. Guyon based her theology of abandonment on the scriptural reference found in I Peter 5: 6-7 that reads, "Humble yourself therefore under the mighty hand of God, that in due time he may exalt you. Cast all your anxieties on him, for He cares about you." In this abandonment, the human soul melts with a spiritual simplicity and becomes part of the living God. Guyon believed that this abandonment included losing all concern about personal reputation and appearance of propriety. Guyon calls this being "lost in God." The Holy Spirit cuts away any part of the human life that is not of God.

Guyon described these operations of the Holy Spirit as mystic, meaning "secret and imperceptible."[32] The believer has a mystic death when becoming a martyr of the Holy Spirit, and the final outcome of this death is when "truly mystical souls, have no power of their own; all their strength is in God alone."[33] Guyon named this spiritual process as an annihilation that is grounded in the idea of indifference. Based on God's gracious generosity to all humanity, the person can be indifferent to whatever happens. The believer can even be indifferent to eternal salvation, because God makes loving decisions.

In annihilation the operation of the Holy Spirit destroys a person's selfishness and self-centeredness. Very few people allow God to complete the annihilation. To endure annihilation involves a spiritual journey that will involve persecutions and unexpected occurrences. Guyon described this journey as an intense personal struggle between the divine love (also called pure love) and self-love. The former dominates the latter only with great difficulty. The struggle for annihilation in the interior person goes through identifiable stages. In the first stage, self-love is pushed out of the higher human faculties such as intelligence, reason, judgment, wisdom, strength, and deliberation or choice. After this struggle is fought successfully, then self-love can only live in the senses which Guyon called the lower faculties. Guyon offered the metaphor that self-love first fails in the higher faculties and then is chased to the inferior part of the soul which she defines as the senses. While in the senses, self-love causes confusion until pure love, still fighting for complete domination, vanquishes self-love from even the senses.

To described annihilation, Guyon refers to what she names the martyrdom of the Holy Spirit, i.e. that the Holy Spirit annihilates those willing to bear a testimony for God.

She stated that the vast majority of human beings need the compassion of a merciful God to overlook their sins. An extremely small number of persons are chosen to experience not the mercy of God but the justice of God. Maintaining the Holy Spirit in a person's soul results in the longing for and acceptance of God's justice. These persons who have allowed the Holy Spirit to destroy their selfish will, purify their hearts, and accept God's fiery justice in their lives are recipients of divine justice. To become a martyr of the Holy Spirit requires extreme trials and sufferings. These actions of the Holy Spirit are sometimes wrongfully thought of as an expression of God's wrath or punishment for sins committed. Instead, Guyon believed that the martyrdom is a sign of God's favor and pleasure.

To describe further the state of being a martyr of the Holy Spirit, Guyon offered the term holocaust to explain this way of life. Every Christian is asked to mirror the sacrifices of Jesus. Through divine love God takes the soul as a sacrifice or holocaust offered to the divine. In her *Autobiography* she described this operation of the Holy Spirit.

> This love delights in making those whom it has made one in you the continual victims of its justice. It seems that these souls are made holocausts to be burnt up by love on the altar of the divine Justice.[34]

After this personal holocaust, the person becomes a spiritual leader. Guyon stated that her own innocent sufferings prepared her to become the spiritual mother of many, saying that her sufferings were used by God to nourish many other souls.

Following the process of annihilation, the Holy Spirit begins the work of divinization which is when the human person becomes one with the essence of God. In *Spiritual Torrents*, Guyon writes that the believer possesses a

> state of deification, in which all is God. . . God does not divinize the soul all at once, but by little and little; and then, as has been said, He increases the capacity of the soul, which He can always deify more and more, since He is an unfathomable abyss.[35]

Once the union between God and the believer is consummated, little difference exists between God and the person. Guyon described the relationship between the soul and God as "God is she and she is God."[36] The believer becomes one with the Spirit when the process of divinization is complete.

Guyon refers to these rare souls as "other Christs." She writes in her *Commentary on the Song of Solomon*:

Introduction xix

> The souls of whom we now speak are other CHRISTS, which is the reason why we perceive in them less the features of the saints; but if we seek for the marks of the Lord Jesus we shall find them most clearly there.[37]

After the annihilation and divinization, the person knows spiritual exaltation. Guyon stated that God builds on human nothingness. When the person accepts this nothingness, God uses this foundation for creating the mystic transformation into the reality of Christ. Guyon's example for this is Mary when she asserts that God has "exalted those of low degree." (Luke 1: 52) Guyon believed that her personal annihilation and divinization were accomplished during her time incarcerated in the Bastille. She came to live in a state she described as naked and simple in which her inner state had become unified with God.

Both individuals and churches may know the process of divinization. In Guyon's commentary on *Revelation*, she stated that the church is beginning an era when the church reacts to a new infusion of the Holy Spirit. The church will flourish under the inspiration of new, Spirit-directed leaders. In Guyon's history in *Bastille Witness* the authorities searched for signs of this new church so that they could destroy it.

The image Guyon used for the work of divinization is that of an apostolic state, a person who believes in Jesus as did the first disciples. Guyon believes that the annihilation of chosen souls such as Abbé La Combe and herself also redeems other human souls by participating in an apostolic state. Guyon described this state in this way.

> Our Lord made me comprehend what the apostolic state was, with which he had honoured me; that to give one's self up to the help of souls, in the purity of his Spirit, was to expose one's self to the most cruel persecutions.[38]

As a recipient of annihilation, the believer receives spiritual gifts and a place in God's plan of salvation. In *Bastille Witness*, Madame Guyon elucidated her understanding of annihilation and divinization in clear terms. Her hope is that, "We must then allow the Spirit of God to act in us."[39]

The Roman Catholic Church's Inquisition charged Madame Guyon with heresy. Guyon's book *A Short and Easy Method of Prayer* was a target of these charges, primarily because of her ideas about the easy availability of the path to God. Professional theologians disputed about the difference between acquired and infused contemplation in her theology. Madame Guyon attempted to answer their concerns in her later writing in *Justifications*. She said in *A Short and Easy Method of Prayer* that everyone should take the path of prayer and communion with God. She named this the "Prayer of Simplicity," a traditional name for acquired contemplation in which a person understands truths that cannot be discovered through human reason and discourse. Yet this prayer depends on the initial human efforts and so participated in what is called acquired or active contemplation.

In her Biblical commentary on the Song of Songs, Guyon described the experience of infused contemplation, a way that is only open to certain individuals. Through this prayer initiated by the Holy Spirit, the person begins to know God as the Beloved who desires union with the human soul. At first the person finds God pouring the divine essence into the human powers of memory, understanding and will. As the person continues on the path of Jesus which contains persecution and hardship, he or she begins to know union with God from the depths of the human heart. Madame Guyon acknowledged her influence by St. Teresa of Ávila who believed in a similar infused contemplation.

The gift of infused contemplation was received into the human life in many ways. Guyon believed in solitary prayer in which the divine was received into the soul. She also advocated regular church attendance. In addition to these spiritual practices, Guyon stated that God communicated many warnings and blessing to her through her dreams. She faithfully recorded her dreams and the interpretation she received about this dreams. In *Bastille Witness*, she received dreams while incarcerated that helped her understand the very complex situation in which she struggled to survive.

Scholars divide about the judgment of Madame Guyon's ultimate religious persuasion. She has been seen as an incipient Protestant who advocated a new religious freedom in the Roman Catholic Church. An influential nineteenth century translator, Thomas Cogswell Upham, declared her a Protestant.[40] Indeed, many influential Protestant Nonconformists claimed her as one similar to them. For example, William Cowper and John Newton (the author of the hymn "Amazing Grace") extolled the benefits of reading Guyon's theology, particularly her poetry. Both her publisher, Pierre Poiret, and secretary, Chevalier Ramsay, were Protestant. According to the *Supplement to the Life of Madame Guyon*, she discouraged her followers from converting to the Roman Catholic Church.

Yet Guyon herself believed that she participated in the mystical Roman Catholic tradition of canonized saints. These influences include St. Francis de Sales, Madame de Jane Chantal, Thomas à Kempis, Catherine of Genoa, Catherine of Siena, and Teresa of Ávila. Her theology of the supernatural operations of God that both annihilate and resurrect the believer places her in apophatic mysticism in which the believer waits with an emptied self and trusts that God will fill this. Another reason for placing her in this tradition of Catholic mysticism is that Guyon believed that the major reason to allow these operations of God was to avoid suffering for sin in purgatory. Most Protestants do not accept the idea of purgatory, a place of divine purification that is neither heaven nor hell. Guyon's claim then of being fully influenced by these Roman Catholic saints and building on their works seems justified. Indeed, Guyon argues this at length in her work *Justifications*.

At the end of *Bastille Witness*, Guyon asserted that she no longer had human desires. In stating her lack of desires, Guyon emphasized her profound participation in the will of God, calling this experience the divine motion. When divinity crowned the human soul, the human gradually began to lose self-will and grew to love God alone. This changed the very human being into a new creation. After the resurrection, the believer's soul now lived in the reality of God and did not experience distracting human desires that separated the soul from God.

Guyon called this new creation the full participation in the apostolic state where Jesus was entirely present to the believer. The person knew Jesus and the interior inspiration of divinity, but could not see Jesus with the physical eyes. After becoming part of the apostolic state, the believer had new capabilities of communication and love that were not dependent upon the physical body. For example, Guyon believed that she communicated with others in the apostolic state, even while she was incarcerated.

Guyon stated that God's Spirit in her suffering accomplished her annihilation, yet the incarceration of aristocrats brought special challenges to the state authorities. Guyon describes her jailors as desiring to please those who brought about her punishment, yet they knew that frequently these aristocrats would be released at some point. Aristocrats enjoyed some privileges. Guyon was allowed to send and receive some letters. She was allowed to have two devoted servants while in the Vincennes. Later these servants with whom she shared friendly emotions were removed from her at the Bastille. In the Bastille, the authorities placed two women to watch her at all times. Both of these women died and led to Madame Guyon's request to now be alone. This request was honored.

Yet even though her aristocratic heritage brought some amenities, Guyon describes a desolate incarceration that included a dungeon room without light in the Vincennes with no guards or officials available in the nighttime. While at Vaugirard, the nun beat her on the face frequently. At the Bastille, she spent time without furniture in solitary confinement. She described listening to the cries of others and no one responding. So while some communication and human company mitigated the conditions of incarceration, Guyon describes her imprisonment under the French authorities as one of difficulty and suffering.

Support for the horrific conditions that Guyon and her servants were kept in comes from scholar Geoffrey Bould. In his book *Conscience Be My Guide: an Anthology of Prison Writings*, Bould published a 1697 letter from Guyon's servant to her brother that she wrote in the Vincennes and had smuggled out.[41] Bould does not identify the servant by name but Guyon called her Marie Delavau. In *Bastille Witness*, Guyon talked of the comfort and strength that she obtained from her relationship from Delavau. In her letter, this servant shows her understanding and appropriation of Guyon's theology. She writes,

> There is but little danger of my getting away from the prison of Vincennes, where I have been confined twice. I have been in prison this last time nearly three years. Whether I shall ever be released again in this life, I know not. Perhaps I shall have no other consolation in this life than what I find in suffering. I am not allowed any materials for writing; nor is it an easy thing for written communications to pass in and out of my cell. Unexpectedly, however, I obtained some sheets of paper; and, using soot instead of ink, and a bit of a stick instead of a pen, I have been enabled to write this. . . . I feel for those who have

afflicted and persecuted us. I indulge the hope, that God will, in time, open the eyes of those among them who are upright, but have acted wrongly from false views. It is my desire, especially, that they may be led to understand and appreciate the character of Madame Guyon. We are now separated from each other; I am in this prison alone, she in another place; but we are still united in spirit. The walls of a prison may confine the body, but they cannot hinder the union of souls.

Madame Guyon's theology of spiritual annihilation received widespread acceptance. Abbé Gautheir writes that "the one that would comprehend the annihilation of Jesus Christ in the holy sacraments comprehends also the annihilation of Madame Guyon and her godliness."[42]

The *Bastille Witness* completes the history and theology that Madame Guyon began with the writing of her *Autobiography*. Guyon relates the fulfillment of her own annihilation with her experience incarcerated in the Bastille. Also, in *Bastille Witness*, Madame Guyon clarified some of the history of the Great Conflict. She explained that her persecutions were caused because Bossuet and others aimed at the destruction of her friend Archbishop Fénelon. She writes, "As soon as the matter had been adjudicated in Rome, they stopped interrogating me."[43]

Both Fénelon and Guyon understood that the treasured doctrine of the divine right of kings was crumbling and looked ahead to a different age. In this age God would work through both men and women, both lay and ordained. Guyon and Fénelon accepted that different church structures and denominations would rise and flourish. In the *Bastille Witness* we catch a glimpse of these two individuals striving to actualize a vision for a different society, even as they work in the tightly controlled world at Versailles. That both Fénelon and Guyon's writings remain well read in the postmodern era testifies to the power of their vision for the future. They recognized changes that would later create a new society.

This detailed look at the inner structure of the French penal system also reveals much of the workings of a transforming French culture. During the reign of Louis XIV, early signs of the coming Enlightenment are seen in the changing legal system. In this document *Bastille Witness*, these incipient influences are seen in their early stages. Some of these new powers are rational thought that changed the legal system, a leaning towards gender equality that ended impassioned witch hunts, and a spiritual belief that supported the gifts of male and female, lay and ordained. Madame Guyon's vast influence in the Enlightenment, Romanticism and the church community is revealed in the *Bastille Witness*.

Madame Marie-Louise Gondal's discovery of this French manuscript offers many answers to long unanswered questions. This new light shed on the history of the formerly disgraced Madame Guyon allows attention now to be focused on her rich and unique theological contribution in the area of spiritual annihilation and divinization.

Introduction xxiii

NOTES

1. Most of the information about Madame Guyon's life comes from her *Autobiography*. For more detailed information, see *The Complete Madame Guyon*, (Brewster, MA: Paraclete Press, 2011).

2. Gondal notes that Abbé Enguerrand published *Instructions pour les personnes qui se sont unies à l'esprit et à la devotion perpétuelle du Saint Sacrement* [Instructions for persons who are united to the spirit and perpetual devotion to the Holy Sacrament], Paris, 1673. He died in 1699 (Gondal, Récits 45, n19). See also Millot (28).

3. The scripture that states the belief of God within is Luke 17:21 "The Kingdom of God is within you."

4. *Autobiography*, Vol. 1, 152-153.

5. Madame Guyon's half-brother, Abbé de La Mothe introduced Abbé La Combe to Madame Guyon. Both of the priests were part of the Barnabite order. Later Abbé de La Mothe began the proceedings that led to the Inquisition for both Abbé La Combe and Madame Guyon.

6. The Nouvelles Catholiques was a newly founded religious community formed from converted Protestants. Guyon lived here at the invitation of the Bishop of Geneva D'Aranthon. This community suffered from financial problems, but Guyon's powers to help this situation were limited because she had given much of her money to relatives and placed other financial resources in trust for her children.

7. Guyon, *Autobiography*, Vol. 2, 41.

8. Guyon, *Autobiography*, Vol. 2, 164-165.

9. Guyon, *Autobiography*, Vol. 1, 96.

10. In Quietism, the believer waited in quiet while waiting for the Spirit of God to fill their heart, mind and soul. The person abandoned all of their being to the divine and trusted the Spirit of God to guide them. Molinos led a popular movement in Rome where thousands would wait in quiet for the coming of the Holy Spirit.

11. A *lettre de cachet* means a letter of the sign. This official letter was signed by the king and countersigned by a state official. A *lettre de cachet* offered no details about the incarceration but briefly stated the order that was to be obeyed. Madame Guyon's *lettre de cachet* was countersigned by Bishop Bossuet.

12. Duc de Louis de Rouvroy Saint-Simon, *Memoirs of Louis XIV and his Court and of the Regency,* vol. 1, New York, P F Collier & Son, 1910, 114-115.

13. ibid., 112.

14. François de Salignac Motte Fénelon. *The Maxims of the Saints explained, Concerning the Interiour Life to which are added Thirty Four Articles, by the Lord Archbishop of Paris, the Bishops of Meaux, and Chartres, (that oc-*

casioned this Book,) also their Declaration upon it. London: H. Rhodes, 1698, 223-224.

15. Guyon, *Autobiography*, vol. 2, 314.
16. Guyon, *Autobiography*, vol. 2, 321.
17. *Supplement to the Life of Madame Guyon*, 92.
18. *Supplement*, 92.
19. *Autobiography*, Vol. 2, 228.
20. *Bastille Witness*, Chapter One, 6
21. Madame Guyon respected the Paris Police of Chief de La Reynie's integrity and honesty. She requested that her case be sent over entirely to the secular authorities and appealed to Madame de Maintenon for help with this. Her requests were denied. She experienced ecclesiastical interrogations in both of her incarcerations and believed that they were not as fair as the police interrogations in the Vincennes. While in the Bastille, the new Paris Chief of Police M. d'Argenson interrogated her and attempted to prove that she was dishonest. Guyon confronted him about an untrustworthy witness. Madame Guyon said that she would have stayed in prison except for the suffering caused by the interrogations in which they tried to trap her in her own words to prove her guilty of any crime.
22. Anonymous Author, "Supplement to the Life of Madame Guyon" translated by Nancy James in *The Pure Love of Madame Guyon: The Great Conflict in King Louis XIV's Court*, (Lanham, Maryland: University Press of America, 2007), 93.
23. Bossuet, Jacques Benigne. *Quakerism á-la-Mode*; or *A History of Quietism*. London; T. Martin, 1698, 12.
24. ibid., 16.
25. ibid., 60.
26. Guyon heard about the judgment of Fénelon's *The Maxims of the Saints* only through the ecclesiastical authorities and interrogators. She believed that the church hierarchy was aiming at Fénelon and trying to destroy him but using her as a means of accomplishing this. She said she tried not to say much about any of her friends during the interrogations. She did not describe feeling any pressure about this but said that she considered all people involved with this situation as an instrument of God for her perfection.
27. "Proces Verbal de L'Assemble de Messeigneurs les Evesques de la Province de Toulouze, Tenue par l'Ordre du Roy a Toulouze au Palais Archepiscopal le septieme jour de May l'an 1699." Paris, Francois Muguet, 1699.
28. Nancy Carol James, *Pure Love of Madame Guyon*, "Supplement to the Life of Madame Guyon," (Lanham, Maryland: University Press of America), 101.
29. Guyon, *The Song of Songs of Solomon, with explanations and Reflections having Reference to the Interior Life.* (New York, A. W. Dennett, 1879), 67-68.

30. Guyon, Jeanne de la Mothe. *Autobiography*, Volume 2, 198.
31. Guyon, Jeanne. *The Exemplary Life of the Pious Lady Guion*, (Bristol, J. Mill, 1806), 85.
32. Guyon, *Commentary on Genesis*, 377.
33. ibid.
34. *Autobiography*, 93.
35. Jeanne Guyon, *Spiritual Torrents*, translated by A. E. Ford, (Boston: Otis Class, 1853), 204-205.
36. ibid., 101.
37. *Song of Solomon*, 105.
38. *Exemplary Life*, 325.
39. *Genesis*, 230.
40. See Thomas Cogswell Upham, *Life and religious opinion and experience of Madame de La Mothe Guyon, together with some account of the personal history and religious opinions of Fénelon, archbishop of Cambray*, (New York: Harper & Brothers, 1857).
41. *Conscience Be My Guide: An Anthology of Prison Writings*, edited by Geoffrey Bould. (Avondale: Weaver Press, 2005), 247-248. Madame Guyon is also written about in *Wall Tappings: An international Anthology of Women's Prison Writings, 200 to the present*, edited by Judith A. Scheffler, New York: Feminist Press at the City University of New York, 2002. Dominique Tronc has published Madame Guyon's prison interrogations in *Les années d'épreuves de Madame Guyon: emprisonnements et interrogatoires sous le roi très chrétien: documents briographiques rassemblés et présentés chronologiquement par Dominique Tronc; etude par Arlette Lebigre.* (Paris: H. Champion), 2009.
42. *Supplement to the Life of Madame Guyon* in James' *The Pure Love of Madame Guyon*, 99.
43. *Bastille Witness*, Chapter 4, pg. 8.

Translator's Notes

Sharon D. Voros, Ph.D.

In 1685 Jeanne-Marie Bouvier de la Mothe Guyon published her first book, *A Short and Easy Way of Prayer that Everyone Can Practice Very Easily and Arrive By Means of It to the Highest Perfection,* a treatise on mental prayer and the interior way, prayers from the heart, not rote recitations. This title gives an idea of her writing style. Madame Guyon directs her comments to her readers as if they were sitting right in the room beside her. This conversational, personal approach with a keen sense of spirituality is perhaps responsible for the popularity of her books, but her lack of formal scholarly education, not offered to women, caused her works on spiritual matters to be suspect, confiscated and condemned. Her prison memoir, dated 1707, was never published until the French scholar Marie-Louise Gondal identified the manuscript as Guyon's and published it in 1992. Now simply titled "Relation de Madame Guyon" [Account by Madame Guyon], the manuscript is located now in Vanves, France, accessible through the Jesuit Center Sèvres in Paris. I was able to consult it for the preparation of this translation. Meticulously written in an unknown hand, the original text is one continuous narration, bound in leather, with 199 pages, rather than folios with a stamp from the École de Sainte Geneviève. I have followed Gondal's chapter divisions since they clarify moments of transition in the narrative, such changes in venue for Madame Guyon's incarceration. The final chapter or Epilogue is another version of the ending of the Guyon's autobiography. These memoirs are a personal account, for Madame Guyon wrote these memoirs in her ailing years after her release from the Bastille in 1703. Hence, the reader can anticipate digressions, lapses in chronology, repetition, and allusions to events that she had sworn not to reveal. It was customary in France for prisoners in the Bastille to sign a statement that they would not write about their experiences. These memoirs are the fourth part of her three-volume autobiography which circulated in manuscript form until their publication after her death. The Bodleian Library at Oxford University has one such manuscript, but it does not include her prison experiences.

In 2001, Dominique Tronc published her autobiography and included the prison memoirs as a fourth part. This edition relies heavily on Gondal's notes. Tronc, however, reorders some of the paragraphs, and omits the Epilogue as a variant, since it appears at the end of the three-part autobiography. The advantage of Tronc's edition is that it includes references to letters that Madame Guyon wrote during her incarceration, such as letters to la petite duchesse [the little duchess], Marie-Anne Colbert (1665-1750), the duchess of Mortemart. I have also noted discrepancies between Gondal's and Tronc's editions when they occur.

Madame Guyon's style is typical of seventeenth-century writing with long, convoluted sentences and subordinate clauses with a kind of Ciceronian flare. Marie-Louise Gondal characterizes her sentence structure as "long and monotonous" when writing about other people. Madame Guyon does not hesitate to repeat conjunctions or elongate sentences with digressions. As a translator of her writing style, I was compelled to break up these long, rambling sentences into constituent parts and then reassemble them. My objective is to render her prose into clear English without completely sacrificing the experience of the original French.

We have also attempted to resolve issues regarding allusions to people she dealt with and events. She was understandably cautious when mentioning names and often abbreviated them or simply alluded to the person. Such allusions are common even in Saint Teresa of Ávila as a means of protecting the person. While Madame Guyon mentions her confessor Father La Combe, however, who died in prison in 1715, she clearly states that the letter he wrote against her was a forgery and includes it in this account along with a letter from a priest from Saint-Sulpice, Joachim Trotti de la Chétarie, one of her interrogators who also served as her confessor. I could not locate this letter in the Archives de Saint-Sulpice, so her version of it is probably the only one in existence. In his admonitions of her, in what he perceives as her defiant behavior, La Chétardie writes in an erudite style quite different from her own. We have retained most of Gondal's notes, duly cited, and included additional information helpful in understanding the narrative.

Madame Guyon's discussion of her theology presents another difficulty in translation. She bases her theology on scripture and personal experience. While she never used the term "Quietist" to describe herself, she was accused of being a follower of Miguel de Molinos. She argues that her theology has roots in Catholic tradition and in that sense, she was a follower of Saint Teresa of Ávila, and mentions the false accusations against her in this memoir. She includes such concepts as simplicity, spiritual nakedness, and annihilation, perhaps one of the more difficult of aspects of her vocabulary for the translator, for these terms must be understood in the context of her call for the prayer of recollection and the emptying of self to receive divine grace. Many times, she will begin a spontaneous prayer, digress, and then resume the narration, a feature also seen in Saint Teresa's writing. I believe she is at her best as a writer when she speaks of her own experiences and her joy in the midst of suffering. She also recounts the daily aspects of her prison routine, which included the purchase of her food and wine, some of which was poisoned causing the death of one of her servants. Since prisoners were expected to pay for their own sustenance she gives details on the purchase of food and drink. She was incarcerated in three different places from 1695 to 1703, the Castle of Vincennes, the Convent at Vaugirard, and finally, the Bastille.

Madame Guyon consistently maintained that she was innocent of all charges. She shows her courage and her faith in these prison memoirs, which shed light on her most difficult years. She discusses interrogation practices, the books she read, the criticism of her writings, and the circumstances for her release, Chapter 8 in the Tronc edition but Chapter 7 in the Gondal edition. In the epilogue, echoes for which appear at the end of her autobiography, Madame Guyon states that she never abandoned the Roman Catholic Church. Her memoirs are a testimony to her perseverance and a tribute to her writing ability in those times of stress, incarceration and constant humiliation.

Chapter One

Arrest and Imprisonment in Vincennes

INTRODUCTION

I cannot refuse what you ask, Monsieur,[1] and I cannot refuse what you seem to desire so earnestly, concerning the last times of my life, when God gave me more of his cross to share[2] and when I can say that I was like my dear Master Jesus,[3] in the grip of disgrace and shame. I thought it best to suppress this account of the story of my life that they demanded of me. I explained the reasons for this, which would still compel me to keep silent, if I had not been convinced that what is still necessary to tell you will be for you alone and a small number of my closest friends, to whom I cannot refuse this consolation, if there is any such consolation for them.[4] This is for those who would like to enter into the views and reasons but I am compelled to suppress this for others.[5]

ARREST AND IMPRISONMENT

In the summer of 1695, Madame Guyon attempts to hide from authorities so as not to compromise her friends, for she has failed to convince Bossuet of her good faith. She is found out and arrested, kept under surveillance for three days, and then imprisoned in the Chateau de Vincennes on the outskirts of Paris on December 31st. She undergoes ten interrogation sessions and signs a letter of submission to the Church. However, nothing is conclusive after her interrogations since most of the evidence amounts to interpretations of terms she used in letters that were confiscated at the time of her arrest. For example the term "little church" was considered as somehow a part of the authorities in Rome. Upon her arrival in Vincennes, they also confiscate her wax statue of Saint Michael and imply that she has indulged in Devil worship. Her interrogator, Monsieur de la Reynie, usually in charge of criminal investigations, not spiritual ones, finds nothing substantial in her case, so she considers the matter closed. How-

ever, new requirements from the archbishop of Paris give her new reasons for concern. She is still held and sent to the convent in Vaugirard.

I believe that I have adequately explained the reasons for which I ceased all dealings with the bishop of Meaux [Bossuet],[6] the trouble that he had with respect to the ideas of wealth that he had gathered,[7] and the dissatisfaction of people of importance who, having pushed me to such an extreme, did not wish to deny any of their efforts.[8] I had to be blamed, or to appear to have taught errors. The attestation that the bishop of Meaux had given me, after such a long, rigorous investigation, did not meet the expectation of ideas that they had wished to give about this for those they had named as my friends for the public. I was left with only two alternatives, either to go to a convent in the diocese of Meaux under the care and direction of that prelate,[9] or be pushed into all that the authorities and their violence could make me imagine of the most atrocious sort.

I had such extreme revulsion, and deep in my heart I was so opposed to the first of these two alternatives that I did not hesitate for a moment. My friends foresaw and feared the consequences.[10] I let them know that I believed that God asked me to abstain from any further dealings with the bishop of Meaux.[11] I went to find a place where I could remain unknown to the entire human race, and if God allowed me to succumb to violence, I would regard it as an effect of His goodness, or His justice,[12] since everything was the same to me in His divine will.[13] Some of my friends offered me refuge for which I thanked them. I did not wish to embarrass anyone for a cause that had become so odious that it could have brought dire consequences for him or her.

I believed that under the circumstances in which I found myself, I could not remain safe in the hiding place that I had secured; having had indispensable dealings with some people from the outside since my return from Meaux, I had grounds for believing that they had some knowledge that could be used for my arrest.[14] I attempted to find another place of refuge further away, but that attempt only contributed to what I was trying to avoid.[15] One of my servants had to go often to that house where I wished to stay to arrange to move my furniture. She was recognized by Monsieur [Gilles] Fouquet's manservant.[16] This brought the neighborhood where I had chosen to stay to Desgrez's attention.[17] Given orders to arrest me, he thus discovered my whereabouts.

I had scarcely been there two months, when, during Christmas festivities, the day of St. John (December 27th) 1695, I saw a man whom I did not know enter my room. He asked me if I were not Madame Guyon. I had been in bed ill for quite a considerable time. I answered yes. And after that, he told me that I was under arrest on orders of the king. I answered him without emotion that I was ready to obey and go where the king wished.[18] I got up out of bed after he called my chambermaid, and he gave orders that he deemed necessary for what he still needed to do. He had surprised another one of my maids in the street. She had gone out for some necessary things. He searched her and found a passkey to my house on her, so he used it to get into my house himself, with twenty or thirty people, all armed, that he placed where he wanted. After that, he went up to my bedchamber. That was done with so little noise that neither I nor my other maid heard anything. Desgrez rifled through everything to see if he could not find some papers. There was no nook or cranny left unexamined. He searched my chambermaid as well. In sum, he did not forget anything in full compliance with his duty and the orders with which he was charged.

He led me first to his home where he left me so that I could realize what had happened. I slept there one night while they deliberated over the place where I was to be imprisoned. They decided at last on Vincennes where I was taken with my maids, with orders that I not be allowed to speak to anyone.[19]

A few days after that, Monsieur de La Reynie came to interrogate me.[20] His austere demeanor did not intimidate me. I calmly answered all the questions he asked me. He had a rather long list provided to him with a great deal of care; they wanted to make me talk about the people that had been in contact with me most closely. I answered him in peace in a simple, natural manner without compromising anyone.[21] That interrogation was very long. And although he spoke to me quite honestly, I noticed that he had been forewarned about me.

He returned a few days later and wanted to know about two letters he showed me that Desgrez had found in a drawer of a small table that was in my bedroom. I answered him that they were from Father [François] La Combe[22] and that I had received them a few days before being arrested. These two letters were the subject of several interrogations, for they maintained that they would find despicable things in them. M. de La Reynie,[23] who approached these issues in good faith, knew nothing of the mechanisms that moved that machine. He assumed that all these evils doings were true and that all the interpretations given to him of the contents of those two letters were valid.

Nevertheless, there was nothing more edifying in these two letters that involved only devotional matters. At the end of one of these letters, Father La Combe invited me to go take the waters that were near him. Then, after telling me of the joy he had in seeing me, he added that he would not be angry at seeing "Family." That word stood out as a frightful thing, worthy of the fire.[24] My interrogator had to use all kinds of expressions and circumlocutions to make me understand all the ideas that took shape around that word. And M. de La Reynie exhausted all the abilities he had in catching a criminal off guard in order to extract from me the knowledge that they had made him understand regarding the significance of that word. Finally, I began to understand his intentions, for until then, these terms had been so obscured that I could not imagine what he was getting at, and I said to him: *"Sir, you could have saved yourself, and me also, a great deal of trouble, if you had only insisted on asking me directly about the explanation for the word 'Family' that Father La Combe mentioned in that letter. It is the name of my chambermaid [Marie Delavau] who is here.*[25] *She has served me for twenty years and Father La Combe knows her well."* M. de la Reynie's prejudice was so great that I had to take all the trouble in the world to disabuse him of it, but at last I gave him such proof that he was wrong that he finally gave up and began to open his eyes regarding the rest of the accusations that were not any better founded.

In this same letter there was mention of a woman named Jeannette [Pagère] who was always going to extremes.[26] She claimed she had very intimate *"knowledge"* from me according to which I had been *"ordered."* On that basis, my interrogator wanted to force me to tell him what this knowledge was and what I had been ordered to do. For a long time, I refused to answer such questions that he asked me in any precise way regarding this issue, but in the end, being pushed to the limit, I told him that I refused to answer anything about this matter only because it was to my advantage.[27] *"But you are forced to do so,"* he replied, *"and they order you to do so."* Then I told him that this woman knew that I was very dear to God, and that she had said several things of that sort to Father La Combe, and this was what he had ordered me to do.[28]

There was still something in that letter that seemed to turn M. de La Reynie against me in the course of his interrogations and it was a passage that said, *"The Jansenists are on top."*[29] That statement made me believe that he leaned toward Jansenism, although I was always against it. But I only saw in him righteous conduct and integrity.

In another one of these two letters, there was the statement: "The little Church greets you, persecuted noble lady." It is not possible to examine all the torment and trouble that I had to clarify the meaning of that expression during the course of several interrogations. They understood that I wanted to establish a different Church and that there were abominable and mysterious things involved with it, for which I alone could reveal the secret.[30] I do not know if M. de La Reynie believed it, but there is nothing that he did not try to do to draw knowledge out of me about this so-called mystery. I had difficulty telling him that it was a simple, natural expression to designate a small number of people united in sentiment and charity to be with God in a more particular manner than what is commonly done among other people, or, as Saint Paul said in one of his Epistles,[31] among the same family or the same house. Whatever it might be, the term "little Church" was the subject of a great number of questions, which were, if I am not mistaken, given to M. de La Reynie by people for whom my guilt mattered a great deal.[32] For, according to him, there was too much at stake to have someone arrested over such trivialities.

During the first visits I had from M. de La Reynie at Vicennes, I told him that there was a very sure way to get to know about my life; I begged him to ask the king himself to review my case; it would be easy to learn about my life in detail and it would be easy for him to judge the depth of these things that he was trying to attribute to me.[33] He spoke to the king who found this to be a good idea. And, with this, I entered into detail with him about all the places where I had been, about all the people who had accompanied me, all those whose homes I had lived in and with whom I had dealings, the times, the places, the dates, and under what circumstances; I accounted for all the moments of my life. He told me, after three months of questioning, that they had nothing against me, and that I could remain in my customary tranquility. He added: *"All justice will be rendered to you."* Undoubtedly, he believed this sort of statement to be true.

Finally, after nine or ten interrogations lasting six, seven or eight hours each sometimes, he threw the letters and papers on the table with a kind of indignation and told his clerk in my presence: *"You have tormented this person for so little,"* as if he were angry at having caused me so much pain. He asked the authorities at Vincennes to have consideration for me and led me to believe that I would be freed soon.

He interrogated me for the tenth time during which he asked for my permission to laugh. It was about a popular blue book titled *Griselda* that they had found in my house.[34] I told him all the beautiful things in it and finally he told me that in order to evaluate it, he would buy it that very evening. After that interrogation, he told me quite honestly that I had nothing to worry about, everything would be returned to me, and I would be freed soon.

I would say that during all the time that I was at Vincennes when M. de La Reynie had interrogated me, I remained in a state of great peace, very content to spend all my life in prison. There was so little daylight in the place where I was kept that I could hardly see. It was even necessary to get close to the place where light came from to do my most important work.

I wrote some canticles that the maid who served me learned by heart as soon as I wrote them, so that they would be remembered, and we sang your praises, O my God. I considered myself a little bird that You had in a cage for Your own pleasure and who had to sing to fulfill her state. The stones of my tower even seemed like rubies, for I considered them better than all the magnificence of the century. My joy was founded on Your love, O my God, and on the pleasure of being Your captive. Whatever I thought in composing these canticles, the bottom of my heart was full of that joy that You give to those who love You in the midst of the greatest affliction.[35]

My infidelities[36] disturbed my peace of mind for a few moments, but peace returned quickly, and, I believe, O my Lord, that You only allow that fault in order to make me see the uselessness of our plans and our spirit in similar encounters, and the certainty of being faithful to You.[37] Those who base their lives on human reason will say that one must foresee and plan, for to do otherwise and wait for miracles is to tempt God. I let others think what they want. As for me, I only find security in abandoning myself to the Lord. All Scripture is full of testimony that requires that abandon. *"Place your worries in the hands of the Lord and He will act himself. Abandon yourself to His guidance and He will guide your steps himself."* [38] God does not intend to set traps for us when He says that. He teaches us not to premeditate our responses.

The testimony that M. de La Reynie gave concerning my innocence only served to embitter those people who persecuted me.[39] Not only was I not released, but they did not allow M. de La Reynie, or even Desgrez, to come to see me. For as much as the latter had prejudice against me, so he had misgivings concerning my relationship with M. de La Reynie, in lieu of whom they sent Monsieur Pirot to me.[40] Desgrez, having learned that they did not want him to see me because they did not trust him, assured them that he was very much in opposition to me and seemed to believe all that they told him. He returned then and told me that M. de La Reynie had said to him: *"Let's get out of here. They want us to make that lady guilty and I find her very innocent. I do not want to serve as an instrument of her destruction."*[41] In effect, they gave him another job and I no longer saw him after that. The one who succeeded him acted in a very different way.[42]

A while after that, they sent M. Pirot to me who spoke with bitterness and hostility. He wanted to review all the questioning all over again that I had been subjected to at Saint Mary's by Monsieur l' Official, in his presence, eight or nine years ago.[43] And since those interrogations were very much to my advantage because of the help from my divine Master Jesus, he wanted to change them to make them seem very evil. After having tormented me to the point of making me ill, for there is nothing more violent than what he did to me, he wanted me to tell him all the evils imaginable about Father La Combe. He had never been able to pardon him for a single word that priest had told him before in the presence of M. l'Official: *"You are a doctor in Israel and you do not know these things."*[44] I answered him that I only had good things to say about him and that I would not have gone to confession with him for such a long time, had I recognized the least impropriety in him. M. Pirot became so bitter over this at that point that he lost all control. I have never known a more bitter, tyrannical man. He wanted me to declare that Father La Combe was no longer my spiritual director and that I had no dealings with him. I gave it to him in these terms.[45] Although I had known Father La Combe as a holy man, I consented to never being advised by him again since the archbishop of Paris deemed it inappropriate;[46] in the future I would have no dealings with him, since I preferred obedience over all else.

A short while after that, he returned and told me that he was unhappy over what I had put in that declaration: that it was for obedience that I would no longer have dealings with Father La Combe; they wanted me to put down that it was because he was a dangerous man and a heretic and that dealing with him was very bad and finally that he was a man for whom one must erase all memory with horror. I responded to him: *"Sir, the Father is a saint and a man of an irreproachable life in whom I have always seen good. It would be to speak against my conscience and commit a great sin to testify against him."* Then he answered me: *"They want this from you, without which you will never receive the sacraments."* I told him this: *"It is not pleasing to God for me ever to take the sacraments through a crime, and although I strongly desire to receive Our Lord whom I love solely, I prefer to be deprived of this all my life than to buy it with a crime so black and evil that it would be a testimony rendered against my conscience."*

He made me understand then, with affected sweetness, that I should not expose myself in my resistance to the unfortunate consequences that such resistance was capable of causing me. But to cut short his proceedings, I told him: *"Sir, although I suffer here all that one can suffer because of the continual pain that has overwhelmed me for such a long time along with the harsh treatment they do to make me suffer, I declare to you that I prefer to stay here all my life than to be set free by such a means. Nothing in the world is capable of breaking me."*

It is true that the torment this man put me through, by his ruse and his artifice, made me fall ill every time he came, but they regarded my reactions as of little consequence. At last, I fell into an extreme state. It took me to the depths of continual weakness with a great fever.

The Commandant,[47] completely loyal to the persons who persecuted me, was incessantly occupied in setting traps for me and in catching me off guard with my own words in order to accomplish his mission. He treated me with the worst harshness and even refused me the slightest relief that they usually would give even to poisoners and hardened criminals. He did this more to make a fortune than to oppress me. He made it be known then that I was not really sick, so that I would not have the most necessary things in that extreme state.

I requested a confessor to die in a Christian way. They asked me whom I wanted and I named Father Archange Enguerrand, a Franciscan recollect of great merit, or a Jesuit.[48] Not only did they not want to get anyone but they made this request a crime as well. They did not use any restraint with me and outraged me with words that in time I scarcely could understand. They only let a doctor come after I suffered a great crisis. Only God knows everything I have suffered during this torment and all the ways in which I found myself then. M. Pirot, offended that I had asked for another confessor, refused to come again, which made me very happy, but he unleashed himself very strangely against me.

I hoped I would not see anyone anymore. And I was content, O my God, to stay in Vincennes until the end of my life. My solitude was my delight. I wrote poetry and songs when I felt inspired to it. We sang and we spent our confinement in such a delightful way in spite of the aches and pains of the body, the discomfort of prison, and the rigors of our jailers.

What was most unbearable in that place was that they only came twice a day to my cell, no matter how ill I was, with no help during the night. Once, I was so ill for four hours that my chambermaid thought I was dead. She cried in vain, she called, she was in distress, and no one came to help. As for me, since I was persuaded that it was not human beings on whom I should count in times of distress, this state of affairs did not cause any trouble. But the fright that my poor servant had was an intolerable torment for her, since she thought she saw me dead with no help and that she would have to spend the whole night with a corpse.

Toward the end of my time at Vincennes, they proposed that I see the rector from Saint-Sulpice [Joachim Trotti de la Chétardie].[49] He had been in Paris for a short while where he had considerable status. I did not know him but I believed that he had important contacts with one of the men I held in highest esteem, Monsieur Louis Tronson superior of the Company of Saint-Sulpice.[50] I would find in him what I could not find in the other priest. Nevertheless, I had a certain repugnance regarding the first proposition they made to me. But since they proposed it to me in such a way to make me understand that they wanted it, I had to suffer the consequences, which I could not prevent.

The priest from Saint-Sulpice came to see me then, and he fell to his knees as soon as he came into my chamber; he spent a quarter of an hour there in prayers without saying a word to me. That introduction with such pretense made a strong impression of fear on me, which was only confirmed by what happened next. He told me that he came on behalf of M. Tronson, who took great interest in all that concerned me, and that he was a close friend and relative of his. He wanted to be helpful to me and he did not know why they had sent M. Pirot to me, who was a very hard man. He had examined my book, *The Short Way*,[51] and found it very good, and he had told M. Pirot all of this. All these reasons and the apparent simplicity that he showed, exterior signs of a devout soul, won me over and made me respond to him with great frankness. But, my God, You who know the depths of human hearts, You know how much his words were different from his actions! His first visit was spent in that same manner. I had several dreams that should have made me mistrust him had I stopped to think about it. And I believe that it was the warnings of the Lord more than the dreams themselves. His laughter was somewhat forced, but what he said to my chambermaid began to open my eyes.

Since he knew my maid was greatly attached to me, he tried to take her away from me. He promised to get her a better situation and he seemed touched by the anguish that she had in a place like that prison cell. *"Me, sir, leave my lady? There is no situation in Paris that I want. My lady is worth more to me than that!"* I do not know, in what I report regarding others, if I use these same terms, but they have the same meaning. I reproached her for her response when she told me about it. I told her that he would not stop there, and that if he returned with that idea, she should tell him that it was not appropriate for her to leave me in that place where I was. If I were released and in shape to do so without her help, she could reflect on the goodness that he showed her, but then it would be an honor to abandon me at that point. He seemed content with the response that she gave him when he spoke to her about it again, and she did not doubt that it would come to pass.

A while after that, he proposed that I sign several papers.[52] This is what I feared the most because of the traps they could set for me. He did not fail to kneel in my cell as soon as he came to see me. These affectations were suspect. And I had a lot of experience with them. He told me that he would bring something I should sign in a few days, for these were professions of faith and submission. I told him: *"Sir, since I cannot sign anything without knowing what I am signing; they only have tormented me up to now for terms that are not exact for which I did not know the meaning. I beg you to show M. Tronson what they want me to sign. He should prepare it, sign it, and I will sign blindly what comes to me from his hand."* That proposal seemed to stop him. He told me to reflect upon this.

It is good to know that they had this priest come since M. Tronson also showed me kindness. And they were well delighted that a person who could not be suspect could give such a bad impression of me. Besides, he was a friend of the bishop of Chartres[53] whom they were well pleased to maintain the bad impressions they had given him also against me. And one could not have done it more efficiently than through a man who should seem completely disinterested as this bishop. That plan succeeded just as they had imagined.

The priest from Saint-Sulpice came back two days later and told me: *"You are wrong to ask M. Tronson and you are wrong not to want to sign what he proposed you to do. He will treat you more rigorously than I would have done, and you would have been better off with me regarding this."* I answered him that I stood by my statement and I would remain firm on that. It took him more than two months, and two or three days more, for him to come to tell me that I was losing by allowing M. Tronson to give me orders. It would be impossible to sign what he brought to me on his behalf. I remained firm on that and refused to change my mind about it.[54]

Finally, seeing that I had not changed my mind, he took charge of a letter that I had written to M. Tronson, in which I told him about the trouble that all these signatures caused me that they incessantly asked me to do. Since I did not know the meaning of their terms, I feared that in using them they could infer that I had sentiments contrary to the faith; I begged him to prepare a statement of submission himself that could satisfy the archbishop of Paris and that would protect me from the impression that they tried to impose on the public against me.[55]

M. Tronson sent me a letter, all prepared and written in his hand, and he assured me that it seemed to him that I could sign it in all confidence. The letter did not contain anything that could hurt the holy doctrine the least in the world, nor the solid truths of interior ways. They were satisfied with the condemnations of my books in which expressions could be misinterpreted. This would pardon me abundantly and justify me regarding the meaning of terms contrary to my intentions. This was in effect what I had asked for.

The priest from Saint-Sulpice, in giving me M. Tronson's reply, put this letter of submission in my hands. It said in essence that I had never gone astray from the sentiments of the Catholic Church, my spiritual mother, for which I had always had, did have, and would have, all attachment possible with God's grace all my life. If my ignorance had made me use less exact terms, my sentiments have always been correct, etc. Finally, despite the persecutions they made me suffer, all their accusations depended on those terms. I signed the paper they brought to me.[56]

The priest from Saint-Sulpice kneeled then in his customary fashion and told me that he had been more inspired by me with this signature than if he had seen me do miracles.[57] He told me then that I would have my freedom in a short time.

This was the only thing in the world that I was most indifferent to.[58] For, if I had a choice, I would have preferred to stay in that place where no one could impose anything on me; any discomfort that I had there was better than having my freedom and being subjected every day to new suspicions or becoming the subject of new tragedies.[59] My solitude was so sweet, since my maid was with me, from whom I hid nothing and with whom I could pray or keep quiet whenever I wished.[60] Without the perpetual interrogations that I had to endure, I would have preferred prison to all the delights of this life. For my pleasure can never be in those things, but only in God. The ease of finding Him without being subjected to seeing or speaking to anyone was a great pleasure for me.

The following day after that, the priest who, the evening before, was so satisfied by the statement of my submission, came to see me with the severe look of a school master. He told me that they were convinced that all I had signed was mere hypocrisy. They no longer had any regard for me and they were not satisfied with it. I told him that I could not do any better and that the only thing to do now was to leave me there in repose.[61] I resigned myself to ending my days in prison.

But God was not yet content with what I was suffering, nor were my enemies (who called themselves that, for I can only consider them as instruments in the hand of God).[62] Nor were my enemies, as I was saying, content with what they had made me suffer.[63] Since I had not heard mass on Easter Sunday, and had not been to mass since I had been there, they took advantage of the desire that I had to fulfill that duty and receive the sacraments as a means of tormenting me further. They consecrated a chapel near my tower. Then they came to tell me that I could not approach the sacraments unless I signed a statement saying that I would have no other Director than the archbishop of Paris and that he would have care of my soul. Very far from finding repugnance in this, I had much joy. And I was satisfied that the archbishop of Paris, who knew me in depth personally, would have more impartial sentiments for me than those who had inspired him to become involved. But, it did not turn out that way, for never, during that time, was he informed in the least about me, as to whether I had a reasonable Christian soul or not. On the contrary, he treated me as if my soul, like that of a beast, ought to perish with my body. That I served and loved God was what they placed little value on, provided that they could denigrate me in the eyes of humanity.

A short while after that, the priest from Saint-Sulpice returned. He did not kneel down to pray any more, but with a look full of anger, he told me that archbishop of Paris was not content with what I had signed with M. Tronson. He was offended.[64] I had to sign another letter of submission without which they would not give me the sacraments. I asked what fault there was in the letter from M. Tronson. He answered that it was because it was signed by the archbishop; they only wanted a letter with the same content, but I had to write it in my own hand and sign it. I said that it would not be difficult. All they had to do was give me M. Tronson's letter. Then I would transcribe it and sign it.

They came back a while later and brought me one all prepared. They said it was transcribed from M. Tronson's letter. I did not want to sign it without seeing the original, but they refused to show it to me.

I admit that nothing in the world was more painful to me than those signatures, for, as I did not know the meaning of their terms, I was always afraid that they would slide in one that would make it seem different than what I thought, and I would have preferred to die. I saw so many people full of passion trying to catch me off guard and set traps for me, but I was alone with no counsel and no knowledge. I had argued correctly that the bishop of Meaux [Bossuet] had made me sign one letter and that I would sign the same thing; since it concerned the same topic. M. Tronson's letter was almost the same. The archbishop of Paris, however, wanted to have his own letter.

Finally, I asked to be able to read it at the very least. They read it to me without giving it to me. But, since I was worried about the trap, and they would not let me read it, I refused to sign that one either.

A short while afterward, they brought me another letter, or perhaps the same one, for me to read. I did not find anything there that said anything more than the others did, at least from what I could judge in my ignorance with the pain I was feeling. They held a sword to my back every day. They asked for letters for the archbishop of Paris that they brought all drawn up that they had to copy, and that was done to torment me.

It should surprise everyone that while the bishop of Meaux treated me always as an ignorant woman who did not know anything at all, they then treated me more harshly than the most expert theologian who had knowingly made errors regarding the most essential points of our faith. This is what I said before the condemnation of my books.[65]

I said therefore: when one writes bad books, one is happy to see them condemned without tormenting the writers, unless they write to promote more condemned books. And yet, how does one deal with them? At the very most they exile them. But I have only erred on a few terms, according to the bishop of Meaux himself, which are not within all the rigor of theology, and since I am not a theologian, and in a way that only concerns prayer, about which they have written more strongly than I, why put me in prison? I have always been submissive [to the Church] with my whole heart. Why torment me for almost twenty years for the same thing after all the submissions they demanded of me? I have consistently declared my attachment to the Church and yet they have never forced me to admit my errors. I always asked that they condemn my books if they found them in error and at least they should leave me in peace after that. I never was able to get a response.

Many times I said to the priest from Saint-Sulpice: *"Sir, if I think in error, please correct me. If I pray in error, please tell me how you wish me to do it, for I have neither an agenda nor a will of my own."* He answered that my prayers were good and that there was nothing to be changed in them. I answered him: *"But if I pray correctly why torment me?"* No response. O my God, it is true that I am a marvel of Your mercy and a misery on my part, for what greater mercy is there than to have me called to be true to the image of Your Son?[66]

I forgot to say that in putting me in Vicennes, the clerk's office confiscated my little wax statue of Jesus and my image of Saint Michael, where they were left for a long time. They asked me where I got the idea for such devotion to the infancy of Jesus and what did "little Jesus" mean?[67] They interrogated me several times on this and on my devotion to Saint Michael.[68] They said such bad things about me and they thought so much about this that they believed that it was because the Devil was in the image and that I honored Saint Michael for that reason. And they said, without spelling it out and without daring to say it openly, that it was the Devil I worshiped. That thought made me shake with horror.[69]

To return to my story, at last, after many trials, the priest from Saint-Sulpice came to make me confess. He said mass and he gave me communion. I took communion then every Sunday and on holidays. They would have been happy to let me stay in Vincennes, and I would have wished to stay there also, but they did not dare to let me stay because M. de La Reynie knew the truth. The priest devised a stratagem to get me out of Vincennes in such a way that they would still be masters of my fate and could dispose of my person according to what was convenient for their own interests.

For that, he had a girl come from Lower Brittany where she was in a sort of religious community that until then did not have an establishment in Paris, although the community had been asking for one for quite some time. He believed that he could not find a more favorable circumstance to attract them there than to propose that I be placed with women for whom he was the Superior. It was a kind of "Congregation of St. Augustine." They have one, two or three sisters in each house. In an instant, they created a community of these sisters in Vaugirard. They placed a sister there with a peasant girl whom they took as a servant. It was in that community that was hastily set up that they placed me when they made me leave Vincennes.[70] But beforehand they took all the precautions necessary to make sure that she and her devoted sisters were there to mistreat me or to make sure that these persons would conform to all their plans.

The priest from Saint-Sulpice came to tell me, with graceful demeanor this time, that he was going to take me home. I let everything be said and everything be done. He had proposed before to take me to the General Hospital.[71] God knows that since I love the poor and humiliation, I would not have had trouble there. But they did not dare do this because of my family. He spoke of sending me to Bourges. I said that I preferred Vincennes. His plan, as the following events showed, was to have me kidnapped on the way and then say that my friends were responsible for the kidnapping. They wanted to catch my friends in my own misfortune. Finally, he came to swear to me that he was going to take me home, but that before that, they would take me to see M. Tronson. He said that so that I would not be shocked at seeing myself outside Paris.

NOTES

1. Although the addressee is unknown, Guyon might be addressing a spiritual director. Another possibility is André-Michel de Ramsay (1686-1743) when he worked as Madame Guyon's secretary. He carried messages between Guyon and Fénelon. This book might have been written before his arrival so the addressee's identity will remain hidden. See James, *Supplement to the Life of Madame Guyon* in *The Pure Love of Madame Guyon* (85-104).

2. Throughout her life Guyon prayed for the cross of Jesus to experience the same suffering as Jesus experienced in his crucifixion.

3. Master or maître is Guyon's preferred title for Jesus (Gondal *Récits* 31 n2).

4. Guyon uses the term consolation as a theological one for an anointing from God that provides strength and comfort. Guyon believes that all consolation comes from the Lord.

5. Upon release from the Bastille, prisoners were warned not to write about their experiences on threat of a new incarceration. Guyon also writes in her *Autobiography* that she did not want to write about this second incarceration out of respect for some state officials and charity towards others whose zeal had made them persecute her. Guyon quotes from I Peter 4: 9, "love covers a multitude of sins," to support her initial decision to suppress this story. For Guyon to enter into the states of others is a sign of spiritual development. Most people are not capable of this form of understanding because it requires interior prayer. So this document is for those who can enter into divine and human states of being.

6. Jacques-Bénigne Bossuet, bishop of Meaux, clashed with François de Salignac de la Mothe Fénelon, bishop of Cambrai, and eventually Guyon. Fénelon defended mysticism in his *Maxims of the Saints* and carried on a lengthy correspondence with Guyon. See James, *The Conflict Over the Heresy of "Pure Love,"* Chapter Four, "Bossuet and Fénelon: Opponents Over Madame Guyon;" Marie-Louise Gondal, *Madame Guyon*; and Marie-Floriene Bruneau, *Women Mystics Confront the Modern World*, especially Chap. 7.

7. The phrase the "ideas of wealth" is the literal translation for Guyon's work. She seems to be avoiding saying much directly about the famous Bishop Bossuet. Yet from her other writings, her meaning seems to be that he had many motives for her incarceration. Some of these motives were a desire to please Madame de Maintenon, hopes to be the next Archbishop of Paris, ambitions to become a cardinal, and the desire to destroy Archbishop Fénelon whom he thought of as an enemy. Bossuet also believed that God had put him in this powerful position to accomplish the destruction of all who believed in the heresy of Quietism.

8. In her *Autobiography*, Guyon says that once the charges were made, those who did this feared exposure if the charges were dismissed.

9. Catherine Millot discusses Guyon's confinement in the convent of Sainte-Marie de Meaux while her writings were under scrutiny by Bossuet (92).

10. In her *Autobiography*, Guyon states, "M. Fouquet was the only person to whom I confided the place of my retirement. He told me, at the end of several months, that the change in Madame de Maintenon towards me having become public, those who already had so much persecuted me kept no longer any measure: there was a horrible outburst, and they retailed stories in which they attacked my morals in a very unworthy manner." Vol. 1, 273.

11. Guyon says in her *Autobiography* that Bishop Bossuet abused her in order to please Madame de Maintenon.

12. While in Geneva, Guyon said that she was given the choice between success and salvation or persecution combined with the glory of God alone. Choosing the latter, she writes, "I prostrated myself, my face to the earth, for a long time, as it were, to receive all your blows, O amiable justice of my God, with which from that moment I felt myself inflamed. Strike, O divine Justice, who have not spared Jesus-Christ, God-Man, who gave himself up to death to satisfy you." *Autobiography*, Vol. 1, 285.

13. In this idea, Guyon expresses her theology of spiritual annihilation. She believed that the Holy Spirit martyred those most dedicated to God. The decisions about one's life were made entirely by God.

14. Her description of this decision to hide herself come from her *Autobiography*, vol 2, 323-324. Guyon describes her motivation for finding a secret place to live as, "As I was informed they were about to push things to the utmost violence, I believed that I should leave to God all that might happen and yet take all prudent steps to avoid the effect of the menaces that reached me from all sides."

15. See Gondal, *Madame Guyon* (148) for the different places she sought refuge. She was arrested in Paris on the rue Popincourt. See also Millot (93).

16. Gondal (*Récits* 35 n4) identifies this person as Gilles Fouquet and not Nicolas his brother.

17. Desgrez is the police officer who arrested Guyon on December 27, 1695. See Gondal (*Récits* 36) and Mallot-Joris (363 and 436).

18. Guyon believed that her lack of emotion was due to her spiritual state of living in full surrender to the divine will.

19. Guyon writes in her *Autobiography*, Vol. 2, 324, that she was first kept at the house of "M. des Grez" while they decided where she would be incarcerated. She writes, "The King, full of justice and kindness, would not consent to put me in prison, saying many times, a convent would be sufficient. They deceived his justice by the most violent calumnies, and painted me to his eyes with colours so black as to make him ashamed of his goodness and his equity. He consented then I should be taken to Vincennes." After this place in her *Autobiography*, *Bastille Witness* contains all new information not included in her *Autobiography*. It appears as if *Bastille Witness* was deleted at the end of Chapter Nineteen. The portion left in the *Autobiography* as Chapter Twenty corresponds to the "Epilogue" in *Bastille Witness*.

20. Gabriel Nicolas de La Reynie is chief of police in charge of criminal investigations, not charges of heresy. See Gondal (*Récits* 36 n9) for the number of interrogation sessions as nine from 31 December 1695 to 5 April 1696 that La Reynie conducted at the Vincennes prison.

21. She also desires to be honest about her friends yet she does not offer any information that could damage them.

22. François La Combe (1640-1715), a Barnabite, was Madame Guyon's spiritual adviser or director. He was imprisoned in 1687 and sent to Lourdes, then Vincennes and finally died in Charenton. He was declared insane. See Gondal (*Récits* 37 n10). The Barnabite Order was founded in Milan with Saint Barnabas as patron (Mallet-Joris 183).

23. Monsieur is abbreviated as M. throughout. We will follow that same convention.

24. Bossuet had called for Guyon to be burned at the stake in his book on Quietism. See *Quakerism à-la-mode; or A History of Quietism*, London: T. Martin, 1698, 60.

25. Charles Urbain, Ed., "Une apologie du P. La Combe"(85 n4). See also Gondal (*Récits*, 35 n30). Two women accompanied Madame Guyon, Françoise Marc and Marie de Lavau, whom Urbain identifies as "Family."

26. Gondal identifies her as Jeanne Pagère whom Father La Combe knew in Lourdes where he was first imprisoned (38 n11).

27. Guyon is unwilling to appropriate anything for he self. She is reluctant to answer de la Reynie's question in a way that would make her look righteous. Guyon states in her *Song of Song* Biblical commentary (Whitaker House 49) that her "dove-like simplicity" stops her from trying to appear good.

28. Father La Combe had never resigned as her spiritual director so he could still exercise spiritual authority over her.

29. The two main Catholic movements in France were the Jesuits and the Jansenists. The Jansenists emphasized personal piety, moral reform, and individual introspection. As such, a leader with Jansenist leanings would refuse to persecute an innocent person.

30. France at that time struggled with its growing numbers of Protestant believers. Guyon's friend, Archbishop Fénelon worked in his early career to convert Protestants to Roman Catholicism.

31. This could be a reference to Romans 16:16, "All the churches of Christ greet you."

32. Guyon is referring to Bishop Bossuet and Madame de Maintenon who both desired Guyon to be found guilty of heresy. Bossuet had recommended that she be hanged or burned in his book on Quietism.

33. King Louis XIV had intervened to end Madame Guyon's first incarceration. Through his wife, Madame de Maintenon, King Louis was closely informed about both the life and the accusations against Madame Guyon.

34. Griselda, a poor shepherdess, is a character from the tenth day and the tenth story of Boccaccio's Decameron (Gondal, *Récits* 40 n13). Her noble hus-

band submits her to a series of tests of her faithfulness to him, including feigned murder of their children, divorce, and preparations for his new bride, all of which she endures and overcomes. This theme of the unjustly persecuted wife must have appealed to Guyon since she had this narration in her library. The "blue library" of Troyes published popular editions of novels (Gondal *Récits*, 65 n14). A more likely source is Charles Perrault (Loskoutoff 150).

35. These lines are a direct quote from Guyon's *Autobiography*, Vol. 2, 328.

36. Gondal notes that Madame Guyon attempted to premeditate her responses or "infidelities" (*Récits* 41 n14). However, she had no legal counsel. According to James, Guyon wrote more at length about this "infidelity" in her Autobiography, Vol. 2, 328-329, for she bases her theology of not considering her responses beforehand on scriptures Mark 13:9-11, John 14: 26, John 16:7-11 and Luke 12:11-12. All of these scriptures counsel the believer to trust the direction of the Holy Spirit given in that same hour. "But take heed to yourselves; for they will deliver you up to councils; and you will be beaten in synagogues; and you will stand before governors and kings for my sake, to bear testimony before them. And the gospel must be preached to all nations. And when they bring you to trial and deliver you up, do not be anxious beforehand what you are to say; but say whatever is given you in that hour, for it is not you who speak but the Holy Spirit." Mark 13:9-11. Tronc's edition has an additional paragraph here: "Cette paix fut alterée pour quelques moments par une infidélité que je fis"(889). [That peace was disturbed for a few moments by an infidelity that I committed. That was to premeditate one day the responses that I should make to an interrogation to which I should submit the following day. I responded to it all in error, and God, so faithful towards me and who had me respond to difficult, muddled things with such ease and presence of mind, knew how to punish me for my precaution. He allowed me to barely answer the easy things and remain almost without knowing what to say.]

37. Guyon believes that God builds on our nothingness and not on our strengths.

38. This paragraph from *Bastille Witness* is also found in Guyon's *Autobiography*, Vol. 2, 328. This scriptural reference is in I Peter 5: 6-7. This scripture reads, "Humble yourself therefore under the mighty hand of God, that in due time he may exalt you. Cast all your anxieties on him, for he cares about you."

39. This included Guyon's initial persecutor, her half brother, Father de la Mothe.

40. Urbain notes that La Reynie had a long collaboration with Bossuet and may have had the idea to imprison Father La Combe as a way of discrediting Guyon and Fénelon. His papers are in the National Library in Paris (69 n1).

41. This is an indirect way of stating that they do not believe that Guyon's destruction is the will of God. In Isaiah 13:5, the scripture says that the Lord uses an instrument of destruction to fulfill the divine plans. The fact that de La Reynie refused to continue his prosecution of Guyon gives some support to her

idea that he was part of the Jansenist movement, a belief system that emphasized moral behavior.

42. For more information about the crucial changes that happened in the Paris police system after de La Reynie left, see Ulrike Krampl, "When Witches Became False: Séducteurs and Crédules Confront the Paris Police at the beginning of the Eighteenth Century" in *Werewolves, Witches, and Wandering Spirits: Traditional Belief & Folklore in Early Modern Europe*, Ed. Kathryn A. Edwards (137-154).

43. James (*The Pure Love of Madame Guyon* 34) discusses her detention in 1688 at the convent of the Visitation of Saint Mary in Paris. See also Gondal (*Récits* 43 n16). This detention included the first interrogations she was subjected to concerning her writings.

44. Gondal (*Récits* 43 n17) cites this quotation as a reference to Jesus' comment to Nicodemus in John 3:10.

45. A long struggle had already ensued in Guyon's *Autobiography* about who was her spiritual director. Father La Combe had encouraged Guyon to write her books, which displeased his superiors in the Barnabite order. Previous to Father La Combe, Guyon had dismissed former spiritual directors herself.

46. The former Archbishop of Paris François Harlay de Champvallon died in early 1695. The new Archbishop of Paris was Louis Antoine de Noailles, a man from the nobility who was friends with Fénelon and close to Madame de Maintenon.

47. The commandant of Vincennes is M. de Bernaville (Gondal *Récits* 59 n1).

48. Gondal notes that Father Enguerrand was the Franciscan who recommended that Madame Guyon seek God in her heart. He published *Instructions pour les personnes qui se sont unies à l'esprit et à la devotion perpétuelle du Saint Sacrement* [*Instructions for persons who are united to the spirit and perpetual devotion to the Holy Sacrament*], Paris, 1673. He died in 1699 (Gondal *Récits* 45, n19). See also Millot (28).

49. Gondal (*Récits* 46 n21).

50. Father Louis Tronson had been part of the Issy Conferences that had cleared Guyon in 1695. Tronson was also a former teacher of Archbishop Fènelon. Gondal calls M. Tronson a prudent, moderate man who had Guyon's confidence, including her circle of friends, Fénelon, the duke of Chevreuse, the duke of Beauvillier, and the archbishop of Paris himself (*Récits* 46, n23).

51. Guyon's *Short Way* is the first text on prayer she published in 1683. See Patrick D. Laude (98). The complete title is *A Short and Easy Way of Prayer that Everyone Can Practice Very Easily and Arrive By Means of It to the Highest Perfection*.

52. Bishop Bossuet had attempted to get Guyon to sign papers and she repeatedly refused his request. This is a common situation that Guyon finds herself in. She feared documents and their use by the Inquisition. The French penal

code had changed in 1682, making it more difficult to obtain capital punishment for the charge of witchcraft but it was still possible to obtain this.

53. The Bishop of Chartres and Saint-Cyr, Paul Godet, had told Madame de Maintenon that Guyon was harming the order of her school at Saint-Cyr by her teaching. On May 2, 1693, Madame de Maintenon issued a command that Madame Guyon could not visit Saint-Cyr again. Guyon submitted to this order.

54. Guyon's idea that the secular authorities would be more impartial than the church officials is proven in comparing the treatment she receives from de La Reynie and Desgrez as compared to the intrigues introduced by Father Joachim Trotti de La Chétardie.

55. Guyon was incarcerated inside the Archbishop of Paris's jurisdiction and as such was answerable to him. In her previous incarceration, she had voluntarily gone to the Diocese at Meaux so that she would not be under the previous Archbishop of Paris' Harlay's jurisdiction.

56. Gondal notes that Madame Guyon signed this letter on August 28, 1696 (*Récits* 50 n31).

57. Guyon insisted on understanding what she was signing in all of her incarcerations. Father Joachim Trotti de La Chétardie seems to be employing some levity in this comment.

58. Guyon uses the ideas of spiritual annihilation in this idea of indifference to what happens to her. In Guyon's theology the idea of indifference is based on God's gracious generosity to all humanity. Because of God's goodness the person can be indifferent to whatever happens. The believer can even be indifferent to eternal salvation, because God makes loving decisions. The idea of indifference was included in the charges of heresy against Miguel de Molinos.

59. Guyon is referring to her many personal tragedies including a forced marriage, the death of two children, the incarceration of Father La Combe, and the condemnation of her books.

60. When describing Guyon, Saint-Simon emphasized Guyon's love of solitude saying that she was "as a woman all in God, whose humility and whose love of contemplation and solitude kept her within the strictest limits, and whose fear, above all, was that she should become known." Louis de Rouvroy, Duc de Saint-Simon. *Memoirs of Louis XIV and his Court and of the Regency*. Volume 1, (New York, P F Collier & Son, 1910), 112.

61. Guyon uses this term repose to signify the repose of the soul on God that is like resting on a couch or a bed. Guyon frequently uses this idea in her Commentary on the Song of Songs. This repose brings a tranquil, sweet rest to the believer.

62. Guyon believed that God used all persons to fulfill the will of God. See note 37.

63. Guyon often digresses in her narrative and this sentence is an example of her writing style.

64. It is unclear whether Guyon means the archbishop or the priest is offended.

65. Guyon argues frequently in her *Autobiography* that she was being held to the standards of a highly-educated theologian, although she was a self-educated lay person.

66. According to Guyon, the greatest of God's mercies is to be annihilated by God and hence ready for union with God in this lifetime.

67. Guyon wrote a treatise on the infancy of Jesus, *Règle des associés à l'enfance de Jésus, modèle de perfection pour tous les estats, tirée de la Sainte Écriture et des Pères*, Lyon, 1685 [*Rule for the Associates of the Infancy of Jesus, a Model of Perfection for Every State Taken from Holy Scripture and Fathers*] (Mallet-Joris 691).

68. This refers to the popular devotion to the Archangel Michael. The primary scriptures references for Michael are in Daniel 10: 13 and Revelation 12: 7-12.

69. The priest here is attempted to build a case of witchcraft against Guyon. See Yvan Loskoutoff, *La sainte et la fée* (150-156) for books and images of the Infant Jesus confiscated when she was arrested on December 27, 1695. Among those books were fairy tales of Charles Perrault, plays by Molière, and a copy of the Quijote. See also Ulrike Kamptl, "When Witches Became False" for ways in which the crime d'exception was handled, often involving witchcraft. Karen Newman argues that the *crimen exceptum*, which included witchcraft, was "not subject to the usual standards of proof, interrogation, and procedure, which required a confession or the testimony of a direct witness. No one had to see a crime committed; instead witnesses could testify merely as to motives and effects," *Fashioning Femininity and English Renaissance Drama* (54). Elissa D. Gelfand notes that there is a "paucity of texts by women" incarcerated in this period in France, *Imagination in Confinement: Women's Writings from French Prisons* (15).

70. Gondal notes that this congregation was called Saint Thomas of Villeneuve. The nun in charge of guarding Madame Guyon is Madame Sauvaget de Villemereuc who became superior general of her house as a reward for her efforts as jailer (*Récits* 56 n40).

71. Mallet-Joris notes that this General Hospital also served as a prison for prostitutes (180).

Chapter Two

Behind Closed Doors in Vaugirard

Madame Guyon is sent to the convent in Vaugirard in hopes that she would attempt to escape, which would give the authorities a way to convict her. Joachim Trotti de la Chétardie [1636-1714], the priest from Saint-Sulpice, is put in charge of her as her confessor and interrogator. Servants and nuns are used to spy on her and make depositions against her. Life in captivity in her cell in Vaugirard was harsh: the confined, small space, the appalling atmosphere of suspicion and constant surveillance, betrayals, insinuations, and the unpredictable nature of her confessor. It was, however, the tension between Bossuet and Fénelon that had repercussions for Madame Guyon. She soon began to perceive that danger was imminent. She also discusses her dreams and the anguish suffered by her loyal servants in her service.

On October 16, 1696, Desgrez came to the Vincennes dungeon to take me to Vaugirard. As soon as I saw him, I understood that I had been deceived, for when one is going to be sent home, they simply set you free, and you do not need the help of people like him to do this. I told him that I understood well that I had been deceived. I knew that they were going to take me to some place where they would be master of all the allegations they wished. I insisted on staying at Vincennes, but they would not hear of it. I could not help but shed some tears, and M. de Bernaville[1] told me that he was quite surprised. I did not cry when I arrived, but I was crying as I was leaving. I told him that in these places, they had witnessed my conduct, but that in a place with no witnesses, it would be easy to publicize other ideas about my conduct. It was for that reason that they did not want to place me in a convent. There are too many witnesses, and not all of them want to condemn someone over the allegations that they wished to force me to make. It was for that reason, they told me, that they would never put me in a convent, because I won all of the nuns over and they only spoke well of me. They sent me therefore to Vaugirard.[2]

When I saw that I had only one nun in charge of me,[3] I understood their intentions much better. I told the priest from Saint-Sulpice so, and he assured me his role in the affair was positive. He said I was mistaken and that in three months, they would send me home. Nevertheless, they did not forget at all what could oblige that nun to do her duty well. They promised to make her a superior general of her congregation, although she had never had that position and other women had never been able to live with her. But, provided that they could say something against me, they would not fail to compensate her. The priest, who was able to get a pension out of this affair, gave her money in hand with the justification that it would provide a floor for me in my cell, but he told her to provide for all my necessities and to write them down. They began by buying me poultry, that I never eat, and many things so that they could note down in their books that I was very expensive and extravagant. They could then use this information (as they did subsequently) to discredit me and pass me off as a sensual person. When I asked them to buy me meat from a butcher shop, that I really liked, they were not able to provide it. They made me buy so many chicks that I could not eat them all, so I let them become hens. A great quantity of food remained for them, including the chickens. I bought everything at a very high price.[4]

They put me in a dilapidated cell with daylight coming through a crack, ready to collapse. While I was there, the foundation had to be reworked, because in order to spare the pillars, everything was propped up by a single support. I almost broke a leg stepping onto a loose board. I said not a word, although I saw myself in danger of being buried alive in the ruins of that building. I spent time in the garden as much as I could, and that they considered a criminal offense, as I will talk about next.

When I was in that house, they left the doors open at first and let the rumors spread that my friends were going to help me escape. I quickly understood the ill will behind that behavior and I easily saw that they had some plan to have me escape and then blame my friends or family for it. They could have just as easily put me in a place where no one would ever have known what had become of me. I told the servant girl who kept guard over me that if they came to take me away, I would scream so loudly that everyone would be warned. My friends or my children would never have allowed such a thing, but they wanted me to be taken away to prove my guilt on other things.

I wrote to M. Tronson, a man of admirable integrity who judged others by his own strict behavior. He informed me that he had seen the archbishop of Paris and the priest of Saint-Sulpice.[5] After having informed them on the subject that I believed I must beware of, he was able to assure me that they had no particular plan regarding me that had anything to do with what I was apprehensive about. They only had thoughts of moderation and peace in my regard. That is how he saw it.

But as soon as the priest of Saint-Sulpice saw that he had missed his opportunity, they put me under lock and key. They stopped up the window that looked out over the gardener's courtyard. They blocked off every hole in the garden itself, even the smallest opening high up on the walls that they had heightened. From that time on, they had no restraint towards me. I still had a small gallery that led to some small places. They condemned the door to it. I had nothing more left than my cell and a passage to go into it, since the chimney was caved in. I had to do my cooking in my cell, despite the heat that it caused. The cell had a very low ceiling and was exposed to the sun all day long. They had blocked off the small window that allowed air to come in. All in all, it was uninhabitable there. As a result, I was in the coolness of the garden, although it was very hot. I used to look for shady places.

They then accused me of bringing men in over the walls through M. de La Reynie's garden. The gardener had a difficult time explaining that the door of that house was always locked. No one ever came in and he saw no one climbing over the walls. They tried to say this was true although they knew that it was not.

That nun who watched over me, as I have said, had been forewarned against me in such a strange way that she regarded me as a devil. All the courtesy that I showed towards her only served to offend her. She thought that it was only an attempt to win her over. Since she was bored in that house where she was alone, and she looked at me as the cause of the harshness that they demanded of her, she always rushed me about. She said that the only thing she had to do was to act inconvenienced because of me and she added many obscenities too painful to hear.

The archbishop of Paris showed her much satisfaction regarding the way in which she conducted herself in my regard. He told her that she had more courage and intelligence than all the other religious who had watched over me before, all of this so as not to let herself be deceived or won over.

Often she came to insult me, tell me hurtful things, or hit me on the chin with her fist, so that I would become angry. She treated me as the worst of all infamous people, so that she could make depositions against me and say that I said or did something that could be considered a crime. But, God helped me infinitely, for I am quick and lively and I never lacked patience, by the grace of God.

One night, a horrifying wind blew and broke and overturned trees in the garden. An apricot tree was found damaged in the storm. She said that I had broken it.[6] She summoned several men to serve as witnesses to the fact that I had broken the tree. From my cell, I heard a gardener say that four strong men could not have broken up a tree like that one, since it was the wind. That man added that five or six apricot trees had also been damaged by the wind in his garden, as had that one. That did not stop them from adding this event to the list of my crimes.

Since I had only one chimney, during a day of fasting, the nun had some bricklayers come in around suppertime. The workers said they would have to put out the fire there. She herself came to put it out in front of me. She thought that I would oppose this and that some words would escape me that would reveal my impatient nature, so that she could send a deposition against me. I did not say a word and I went into the garden, happy to miss dinner. I saw a walled-up door in the garden, hollow with some stones on it. I told my servants, who had a difficult time putting up with all of this, to say nothing and to cook some eggs there. That place was rather far from the house, and we used it to avoid giving the nun an occasion to send in a bad report on me. But since she could not provoke me to anger, she made it a point to say that it was still better for her to accuse me of wanting to set fire to the house. Every day there were new accusations.

The priest from Saint-Sulpice kept telling me the most offensive things in the world apart from confession, in order to make me understand that he wondered whether I was a witch or not.[7] But, when he confessed me, he told me that he found me quite innocent and he regarded all of this as a test from God. Aside from that, he was always furious with me. The difference between a priest who acts as God's minister and this prejudiced man was quite remarkable. So, I did not let this difference bother me, and I am able to say that it is a matter of confessing without trouble to one's great enemies. It was to You alone, Lord, that I confessed and exposed my naked soul before Your divine eyes.

He made it a point to tell me that he wanted me to read the newspaper. I resisted as much as I could over the difficulty in having it sent, and the little time that I had to read it. He insisted on it. Once he sent me the *Gallant Mercury*.[8] I did not know where this would lead. I refused to read it again. He withheld communion from me because of my disobedience. He then asked me if I wanted a blue bird that my daughter had sent me, that was at his home.[9] I really believed that it was a bird, and since I like them, I asked him to send it to me. It was a small book of fairy tales. That event was put down along with the rest of my crimes. He also said that I threw letters over the walls.

I had ghastly dreams about him. Sometimes, I saw him vomit some black substance on me. Other times, it seemed to me that Our Lord made him remove his habit and put another filthy one on.

He came to tell me one time that if M. de Cambrai [Fénelon] had not written that book, I would have had my freedom. Other times, he told me that Fénelon's book was against me.[10] I never heard him say even one true word, or use the same meaning twice, for they were always distorted expressions. He often muttered between his teeth like a man who is threatening and does not want to say clearly what he is threatening about. Sometimes he wanted to know firsthand to whom I had given the attestation form from the bishop of Meaux so that he could try to get it back. Then, he led me to understand that they had no regard for my submission letter.

When I first saw him in the beginning, I gave him a letter for M. Tronson, in all confidence. He swore to me as a priest that he would give it to him without letting anyone see it. He took it to the archbishop of Paris, who was very angry with me. Then in speaking to me, he stopped short and at last led me to understand that he had shown the letter to M. Tronson.

The more I confided in him in the beginning, the more my heart was pressed, and I believed that this confidence in him did me harm. All that concerned my faults and my misery, I revealed willingly with simplicity. I said sometimes, "O my God, if You want me to provide a new spectacle to men and angels, may Your holy will be done! All that I ask is that You save all who belong to You and do not permit them to be separated from one another. May powers, principalities, etc., never separate us from the love of God who is in Jesus Christ.[11] In my particular case, what does it matter what men think of me! What does it matter that they make me suffer, since they cannot separate me from Jesus Christ who is inscribed deep in my heart.[12] If I displease Jesus Christ, though I pleased all men, I would then be less than mud. May all men then despise me and hate me, provided that I am agreeable to Him! Their blows will perfect all that is defective in me, so that I can be presented to Him for whom I die every day, until the time when He comes to consummate this death. And I pray, O my God, to become a pure host in Your blood, so that I may soon be offered to You."[13]

In the month of March 1697, I had the impression that the king was dying and would not last beyond the month of September. I told this to the priest from Saint-Sulpice in my characteristic simplicity, and I begged him to tell it to one or two of my friends, for whom I believed it important to know.[14] A few days later, I realized that God had perhaps allowed this impression to come about in order to discredit me in the mind of the priest. I had no trouble because of this and I found myself ready to display humiliation and all the confusion that I would have to endure amid the prejudice that this priest had against me, if it so happened that I was mistaken. God knows how much that faithfulness cost those still alive themselves and what agonies our nature suffers regarding this before we reach certain death as a result, a death that God requires for souls He wants completely for himself. If similar things happened to me and I were in a similar situation, I would still say the same things. But the priest from Saint-Sulpice was far removed from understanding such simplicity. When I made some effort to extend confidence to him, I felt that he did not get it into his head what I was telling him. Most of the time, he did not hear me because of his lack of intelligence. And my heart felt no correspondence there.[15]

I had three small crosses in the garden and I had written there: I go from cross to cross and thus I spend my life. They turned this too into a crime. I practiced Lent with fire and blood, although I was quite ill, even before beginning it. But, I had the courage to observe Lent whatever it might cost my life. Though rather poorly nourished and lacking provisions, and since the Sunday before Lent, I could not get over a fever. Not only did they not propose that I cease Lenten practices, but I fasted entirely during that time. Even a great pain in my eyes and throat along with a fever, a cough and a violent headache could not convince them that I needed other nourishment. But I scarcely noticed it as I was in the will of God. I would have been more sensitive to the order that was given to that nun to not have any priest come to me even in death, if the will of God were not preferable above all other things.[16]

There were moments when the priest from Saint-Sulpice seemed to have some compassion for my state. He spoke to me with such sweetness, but either because of inconstancy or weakness for people who took an interest in my ruin, it did not last long. He made a thousand propositions to me, each one more painful than the first. He affirmed these things with horrible sermons on them. Afterward, it was just the opposite. What afflicted me sometimes in the extreme was that I was forced to confess to a man who oppresses you and declares that he is your cruelest enemy. Sometimes they treated me as a scandalous person, a hypocrite, and a witch. Then, they said I committed crimes in Bretagne, where I have never been, which they nevertheless maintained openly. The priest urged me to declare my magic spells.[17] The piquant haranguing that he did to me regarding the people who knew me afflicted me more than all the rest. He pretended to confess me without letting me take communion to make me understand that he acted with knowledge of my guilt. It was sometimes an intolerable anguish to be forced to confess to him. And I found that it was a kind of ungodliness to force me to confess since he believed nothing of what I told him. I confess that this was one of the things that I was most sensitive to.

One day, he sent a man of his with the parents of one of the servant girls who attended me, with the intention of taking her away from me, but she put up such a great cry that they did not dare to carry out this plan in broad daylight. The nun who guarded me was in on the conspiracy and had separated her skillfully from her companion, out of fear that she would go to her aid. Afterwards, he asked her to leave me but the poor girl was not inclined to accept any of this.

A few days later, that same nun came into my cell to board up the only window that I could get air from. I found myself reduced to a single room, where I had to cook, wash dishes, and do all the rest. The girl who was there, for I had gone down to the garden, told the nun that she could not stand my being cooped up in a stifling cell and since I was not there, she could not allow the window to be blocked up. The nun came to find me in the garden with the fury of a lioness. I got up to greet her. She told me what she had come for. I responded to her, with all the courtesy that I could muster, that since the priest had come, I would do anything he ordered without question and that was what was proscribed for me. She screamed like a fishwife as she held one hand on her head and put the other hand on my chin that she was well acquainted with. She said that she knew who I was and what I knew how to do. She had been well instructed and said that I did not know how knowledgeable she was. All this was accompanied by gestures full of threats and violence. I told her sweetly that I was well known by persons of honor. "*What?*" she replied, "*You say that I am not a person of honor?*" And she said all of this with horrifying rage. I answered her without raising my voice: "*I mean, Madam, that I am known by persons of honor and I will let the priest from Saint-Sulpice know about your methods.*"—"*I do not recommend that,*" she said to me. "*You will find yourself in deep trouble and I know what I will do.*" There was such a racket and it lasted a long time. She told me the most offensive things to try to provoke me and force me to say something in kind, but my God did not allow it. One must experience these kinds of treatment continually in order to understand how much they irritate one's nature and make it suffer, when not even a word of consolation is allowed. I was always very fair toward that nun and gave her all I thought possible to please her. I do not know if they pushed her to do such things or not in order to get me out of there and have me locked up in another unknown place or make me complain and become angry, or ask for anything. But He for whom I suffered gave me patience and did not allow me to fall apart over the slightest complaint. I did not speak to the priest about what had happened and I abandoned everything to God. Then, I found out later that one of the workers present during this episode said that it was necessary to have some adventuresses kept in that house. I asked the priest to come see me.

And I told him that in truth it was quite enough to be closed in as I was without having to hear such atrocious insults and endure treatments of that sort. If I were guilty, they should try me. But it was hateful to expose me to such outrage. The priest seemed to be angry and left to go to reprimand the nun, or so he said, and forbid her to use such methods in the future. He came back and reprimanded me so strongly that I lost all confidence in him. They had assured me that a person of importance among my friends had come to see me. They found it quite necessary to retell what the archbishop of Paris had done to get me out of Vincennes. They said that all my friends had abandoned me and since I no longer had any protectors, I should expect all the worst. I answered him that he knew better than anyone that I could not see the person[18] that he told me about, given the condition and isolation from view that I was in. I was ready to return to Vincennes if they wished me to. I had not been more cooped up there than in Vaugirard where I was and I would be there at least under cover of these supposed visits that he spoke of. I did not ask for any mercy since I had resolved to suffer everything for God.[19]

Despite the extremes to which he was able to go, he softened his statements then and told me that he wanted to render a service to me, but that he was obliged to speak ill of me sometimes. The bishop of Meaux, in pointing him out, had said, *"There is the man right here! They could not put her into better hands."* He assured me that he would protect me against the storm and that he would sweeten everything, but that he wanted a letter from me, to the effect that he had compassion and that I had reason to praise him. He played all sorts of roles and at last had me write a beautiful letter of thanks, which I did.

The trouble from that nun, of whom I have spoken, came from another sister of the same congregation who had come to spend some time in that house at the beginning. The visiting nun had hate and horrible jealousy against that house, but she seemed to be affectionate towards me and spoke well of me to everyone she met. That nun sometimes treated me very fairly on behalf of the sisters of Paris who were very angry about my jailer nun's way of behaving. They told me that it was her temperament. No one could live with her and they urged me to not let myself go to the trouble that this could make me do.

They then blocked off another door, and as for the window that had caused such a fuss, they were happy to put a wooden trellis over it. Thus, they closed me in at my own expense, for it was my own money that paid for the chains and wall that held me captive.

A while after that, the priest from Saint-Sulpice came to see me to forbid me from taking communion from the archbishop of Paris. With a very serious demeanor, he told me that the Maillard woman[20] had come to see him and had told him details of such compelling circumstances that there was no reason not to believe her. He added that I was responsible before God for all the troubles of the Church and that I had perverted such and such a person and that I ought to show great remorse of conscience. Then he urged me to withdraw within myself, convert, and not condemn myself.

I told him: *"But, sir, after having left everything behind as I have and given myself to God?"* He interrupted me without letting me finish and told me that he knew about witches who had done greater things for the devil than the saints had done for God. Nevertheless, they had converted and had died well.[21] He urged me to take advantage of the charity that he had for me. He stretched out his hand to me and said I should take advantage of the moment. He knew without a doubt that Father La Combe was a second Louis Goffridy[22] who was burned at the stake in Marseille. If I forgave Father La Combe, then he would think that I was the same as he [a heretic]. Finally, he said they were showing great grace to me in allowing me to suffer in the place where I was. I answered him that if they thought I should go to another prison, I was ready to do it.

Regarding what I said, that the Maillard woman was an evil woman, etc., he answered me that thieves always accuse one another and lose their credibility.

For most of the visits that the priest paid me, he maintained this same level of discourse and You gave me the grace, O my God, to suffer everything for Your love. When I sometimes spoke out to tell him the truth or to enlighten him, though I did it as sweetly as possible, he told me that I was carried away and that if I had any virtue at all, I would keep quiet. Then he began his exhortations again regarding how comfortable I was there and that I should confess to my crimes. My only consolation, O my God, is that You see inside hearts. Either You wished to chastise me if I displeased You without wishing to or knowing about it, or You wished to test me.[23] This is always the effect of Your goodness.

During one visit that he made a while after that, the priest told me that the reason why they withheld communion for me was that it would show that I was right if I were allowed to take communion and it would make it look as if they were wrong in treating me as they did.[24]

He told me again that people of honor had told him that I preached outside the walls of the convent. No one was better equipped than he to disabuse anyone of that charge, if he had wished to do so. Proof of the contrary are the intensity with which they kept me in that house and the excessive exhaustion of my body. I still have not been able to move around or even stand up without help for several years now.

A while after that, the priest came back and tormented me in excess to make me confess falsehoods. He told me that I was deluded and that a person under delusions is capable of anything. I answered him that, as far as the delusion was concerned, I only acted in good faith, but that he needed to tell me what my error was. That was all that I wished of him. He was able to remember that I had told him before that I would try to pray as they had ordered me to do, but that they had not given any guidance on this. Thus, I would remain in good faith until they told me otherwise. As for these facts, neither prison, torture, nor death would make me avow falsehoods, but I would say nothing to him just to defend myself. He then said the harshest things to me.

What often caused me great pain was the torment that he caused my servants. He forced them to admit the most erroneous things about me. If they said, "That is not true," they were treated as irascible. If they said nothing at all, they were convinced of my error. The priest had a frightful aversion to one of my servant girls. When she tried to say that an accusation against me was false or that it was not true or even believable, he told her that all of this was proof that she had an evil soul, for he attributed all sorts of evil deeds to her. He then refused her absolution for those deeds.

I dreamed during that time that I wanted to go through a very narrow door but that it was almost impossible to do so.[25] The bishop of Cambrai [Fénelon] told me to go through it and I made such an effort to do so that it appeared I was going to be crushed. He held out his hand to me and I went through but with a lot of pain. I thought in passing that I made the door fall on him and I remained very afraid. But with one hand, he replaced the door and I found myself with him in a very spacious church full of people. When I went outside, I found that everyone was eating leaves from a green oak tree and they offered me some. I refused saying that I only nourished myself with the best meats. They reprimanded me for my bad taste and said that this was what was most fashionable now; everyone else found these leaves very tasty. It is only too true that they feed on oak leaves but they reject the living life-giving bread.[26]

Another time I dreamed that my sister, the religious who was dead, told me: "*Leave this place! When you only live in caves and quarries, living on bread given as alms, you will be happier.*"[27] My heart was prepared for all that would please God to command and I was all too happy to give blood for blood, and life for life.[28]

NOTES

1. M. de Bernaville was the commandant of Vincennes (Gondal *Récits* 59 n1).

2. Gondal states that the reasons for moving Madame Guyon to Vaugirard are not clear (*Récits* 60 n2), although Guyon herself says that it could have been a way of setting a trap for her friends to rescue her and then condemn them as well (Gondal *Récits* 57).

3. Gondal notes that the nun in charge of Guyon was Madame Sauveget de Villemereuc (*Récits* 56 n40).

4. Guyon writes in her Biblical commentary on *Song of Songs of Solomon* that out of misunderstanding non-spiritual people accuse faithful ones of excessive sensual desires. They do this because they do not understand those who thirst for the living God (Psalm 42:2).

5. Gondal notes that this segment corresponds almost word for word to the letter Guyon wrote to M. Tronson on the 27th of November 1696 (*Récits* 62 n7).

6. The nun might have believed that Madame Guyon provoked the storm through witchcraft. This was a common accusation against witches.

7. Throughout her second incarceration, the interrogations are designed to prove Guyon guilty of witchcraft.

8. The *Gallant Mercury* published Griselda and Donkey Skin in 1691 along with tales of Perrault in 1694. Madame Guyon and her companions enjoyed popular fiction (Gondal, *Récits* 65 n14).

9. Madame Guyon enjoyed a warm relationship with this daughter, Jeanne-Marie Guyon de Chesnoy, Countess de Vaux. She was married to Louis Nicolas Fouquet, count of Vaux. During Guyon's final years, she and her daughter remained close. Her daughter was at her bedside when Guyon died.

10. Fénelon, the bishop of Cambrai wrote *Explication des Maximes des Saints* published on January 29, 1697 in which he defends mysticism. He indirectly is defending Madame Guyon's form of mysticism without using her name or making any reference to her writings.

11. Guyon is quoting from Romans 8:38. St. Paul writes, "For I am convinced that neither death nor life, nor angels, nor principalities, nor present things, nor future things, nor powers, nor height, nor depth, nor any other creature will be able to separate us from the love of God in Jesus Christ our Lord."

12. Guyon believed that in divinization, the heart of Jesus Christ became one with the believer's heart.

13. In this passage Guyon is praying to become what she calls "other Christs." Guyon refers to these rare souls in her commentary on *Song of Songs of Solomon*, 105.

14. Spiritual simplicity is one of the main ideas in Guyon's theology. She believed that this led her to abandon all of her life. This included her personal reputation and appearance of propriety.

15. Guyon uses the term correspondence to refer to common beliefs and sentiments among spiritual people (Gondal *Récits* 68 n18).

16. In preferring the will of God over the mediation of the Roman Catholic priest, Guyon reveals what have been identified as her non-conformist Protestant beliefs. She understood this as part of the spiritual tradition of other Roman Catholics thinkers, such as Francis de Sales and Jane de Chantal.

17. This provides more evidence that they were accusing Guyon of devil worship and witchcraft.

18. Proof that Guyon probably had some visitors (Gondal *Récits* 72 n26).

19. Throughout her life, Guyon sought the justice of God and not the mercy of God.

20. The "Maillard woman,"supposedly one of the followers of Father La Combe and Madame Guyon, although she does not seem to know her personally, testified against them (Gondal *Récits* 73 n27).

21. After the Affair of the Poisons that roiled aristocratic Parisian society, few questioned the existence of people who held black masses and performed infant sacrifice. Hence, the priest's statement that these persons involved in devil worship had done more for the devil than saints did for God.

22. Louis Goffridy, a priest who was burned in Aix-en-Provence on April 30th, 1611, believed in the existence of an evil spirit. He was accused of being an accomplice of a woman who was believed to be bewitched (Gondal *Récits* 74 n29).

23. The testing of God is a major theme of Guyon. She asserted that the faithful endured extreme tests to their faith similar to tests of Job and Jesus in the wilderness.

24. In Louis XIV's France it was publicly noted who was allowed by their confessor to take communion and who was not. Speculative questions were asked how Louis could take communion when he had mistresses and was breaking his marriage vows. The priest is aiming at a consistent appearance for those desiring to condemn Guyon. This is accomplished at her expense.

25. The Biblical character of this dream is seen in the image of a narrow door. See Matthew 7:13 (Enter through the narrow gate) and John 10:9 (Jesus says, I am the door.)

26. The dream ends with another scriptural reference to Jesus in the scripture John 6:35, "I am the bread of life." The reference to society conforming and eating oak leaves is a metaphor for propriety in society. Guyon considered propriety as the root of all sin. In the *Song of Songs of Solomon* 2: 4-5, a reference to the banquet of God refers to the nourishment of the faithful with the best foods and meats.

27. In this dream, Guyon is referring to St. Anthony, the founder of Christian monasticism, whose life inspired the conversion of St. Augustine of Hippo. In the mid to late third century, St. Antony lived in caves and lived on bread given to him as alms. In Guyon's dream, the message could be that when she

could become a retired contemplative, she would be happier. This dream can also be interpreted as a foreshadowing for the unexpected solitary contentment Guyon found living in the Bastille.

28. Gondal notes that Guyon is ambivalent about attempting to escape as revealed in these two dreams (*Récits* 77 n32).

Chapter Three

New Trials in Vaugirard

During the spring of 1697, the attack on Fénelon's "Maxims of the Saints" [1697] caused a great deal of controversy. Two opposing tendencies met face to face in public. Fénelon defended the language of the mystics. Bossuet and the majority of the Court argued that mystical language was full of errors regarding doctrine. The entire investigation eventually was taken up by the Vatican. As for Madame Guyon, she found herself involved in criminal proceedings, albeit in an indirect way; she is urged by La Chétardie to confess her crimes and admit her errors. She recalls an attempted poisoning that she managed to foil. The harsh conditions at Vaugirard, however, begin to endanger her health and she loses her eyesight temporarily. She includes here a letter she wrote to the archbishop of Paris in which she asks for guidance regarding prayer and swears to obey him. Instead, she is interrogated about events that happened in 1688 when she was incarcerated in the convent of the Visitation of Saint Mary near the Bastille. If she showed any flaw at all in her conduct, it would be proof that her spirituality was suspect.

A while after that, the priest from Saint-Sulpice [La Chétardie] came to tell me that the archbishop of Paris [Louis de Noailles] had irrefutable proof of crimes that I had committed and therefore, he did not see that they would ever set me free.

I answered him that I did not request my freedom and that I had never requested it, but I found it very strange that after having spent ten months in Vincennes in the hands of M. de La Reynie, a very enlightened man and quite forewarned against me from the beginning, and after so much questioning, they were still speaking to me about alleged crimes. Since the beginning of the investigation against me, I had asked them to examine my life.[1] I had addressed the bishop of Meaux and other bishops and even offered to place myself in the prison of their choosing during the investigation they would conduct. This was the first thing that I requested of M. de La Reynie at Vincennes when he first came to interrogate me. I also asked him to consult the king on my behalf so that this investigation [could] be made [and] the king himself said that my request was just. Then, M. de La Reynie made note of all the places where I had been, all the people who had accompanied me, all the people whose homes I stayed in and with whom I had dealings. Finally, after three months of questioning, M. de La Reynie told me that I only had to remain in my usual tranquil state. They had nothing against me. He said in his own words that *"All will be returned to me."*

The priest from Saint-Sulpice answered me coldly that they had decided to put me in Vincennes. *"But sir,"* I said to him, *"why not put me in the Conciergerie in the hands of Parliament?*[2] *If I am guilty, I do not ask for mercy. For they also punish slanderers. It is easy to suspect a person of crimes for whom all means of defense has been taken away. But in a legal system controlled by Parliament, the witnesses that they are sure of perhaps will speak differently of the accused and the truth at least will be known."* He responded to me, *"You are still in the hands of justice, for it is M. Desgrez who brought you here and you are in his charge. And since the crimes that you have committed do not carry the death sentence, it is more secure to lock you up."*

I told him that I would consent to my being imprisoned if they did not bring new charges against me to serve as a pretext for my confinement. But, I owed it to God, to piety, to my family and to myself to request the intervention of Parliament where everything would be cleared up. He told me that he would speak to the archbishop of Paris. If it had not been for the investigation of the bishop of Cambrai [Fénelon], I would have already been released, he said.[3] I answered him that this matter, entirely unknown to me, would not make me guiltier or more innocent. I told him that if the archbishop of Paris had irrefutable proof of crimes I had committed, as he said, then those alleged crimes would not change their nature, regardless of the outcome of the matter concerning the bishop of Cambrai [Fénelon] that he spoke about to me.

He urged me then to confess my crimes to him and said that God had shown great mercy towards me in having removed me from the temptation to continue my errors. Then, he said that I had no confidence in him. Finally he found it right that they had placed me in the hands of justice, but all had been proven and the archbishop of Paris had no doubt about it.

During that time, a rather bizarre adventure happened to me. I needed wine, so they looked around the neighborhood and brought me a very good one at one hundred francs for the half-barrel.[4] Since I found this a bit expensive, I wrote to a man whose name I shall not mention. I asked him to tell me if I could not find wine at a better price since I had trouble spending so much money. Without answering me, that person sent me a barrel at one hundred écus for an entire cask, or fifty écus for the half-barrel. That seemed extraordinary to me, but I let it pass.

A while after that, when I drank it, I found that it burned my mouth, my throat, and my insides, with such pain that I thought I was going to die. I asked them to summon a man from the village, who seemed to be a very honest man, to see if the wine were not still good to drink. As soon as he tasted it, he seemed frightened and said that only a rogue could have sent that wine here. As for him, he would not want to drink even a quarter of a liter of it since he could not taste it without fear. He said there were things in it that he knew well would burn the insides of anyone who drank it. All this happened in the presence of the nurse who watched over me. She was in despair over having him come here.

They made an innkeeper come from the village who offered to take the wine at a two-thirds loss. He said that little by little he would put this wine through a sieve and he would have some strong cart drivers drink it, after mixing it with other wines, and they agreed with him on those terms. He asked them to leave the wine a few days in a wine cellar where he was. But he found it so bad after having tasted it that he sent for a man who tastes wines in his regions to give it one more test. That fellow first poured it into his hand and smelled it. He then refused to taste it and said, in front of that nurse and several bricklayers who were working there, that it was poisoned wine. He said that even if they gave him as much money as he could keep in his cellar, he would not drink it or even taste it, and it was impossible to drink it without dying.[5]

That young nurse, who heard the whole speech, was quite upset and went to tell the priest from Saint-Sulpice all about it. He told her that if I did not find the wine strong enough, I only had to put less water in it so that I could drink it. She did not dare talk back to him. She came back to find me and told me: *"Madame, though this is excellent wine, since it makes you ill, you should not drink it, but if you want to sell a cask of it for two coins, they will take it to mix it in with an amount of other wines."* I told her that getting twenty francs for fifty écus was not worth the trouble and that since the wine was so excellent, the priest should keep it. I was not angry at leaving that thorn in their foot as a way to escape such tyranny.

That nurse did not dare have the priest taste it and said she did not have permission to do so. But, on the other hand, they could not get out of this situation without letting him taste it. This situation remained under those terms for some time. At last, they came to fetch it one night and they exchanged it for a watered-down wine that was not worth very much. I let them do anything they wished and abandoned the consequences to Providence.

More than three weeks after having drunk the little bit of wine that I spoke of, I still had my tongue, throat, pallet, and chest all scorched. I thought I was going to die one day, for I suffered terrible pains in my intestines. Finally, after I drank water, that great fire subsided, and I found my normal state again. That nurse seemed distressed over what had happened to me.

Such a great rush of emotion sometimes took hold of me, when I saw myself in such hands, that I was ready to suffocate from it, but I was not less abandoned to God. I suffered everything without saying a word. Often, I pretended not to see things. They called my patience madness. If I was fearful that they were trying to implicate me in something, since from the beginning I had had such an impression of all this, they looked on it as my latest raving. Thus, the slightest word was seen as a crime; silence and patience were seen as just the contrary.

One day, the priest from Saint-Sulpice told me a word that seemed frightful for a man of his character. It was this: they would not take me to trial because there was no justification to have me executed.[6] Then, changing his mind about it, he added: *"But it is true that they can always mete out a punishment to fit your crime."* He had sworn to me on his share in paradise that I would be there for only three months and that they would not make any more accusations against me. My witness and my judge are in heaven. They can manipulate men, but who can shy away from the eyes of God?[7]

One thing that caused me a lot of distress was whether after so many things had happened because of the priest from Saint-Sulpice, I still had to confess to him. And I believed that I should not have to do this. It seemed to me that there was something shameful in having to go to confess to a man who suspected me of crimes every day and from whom I never heard a word of truth.

I almost lost my sight during that time, and since I could almost no longer read or work, I lost the only recreation time I could have. I sometimes knitted but rather poorly, since it was the only kind of work I could do because of my eyesight. To reward the work that the woman who tormented me did, they made her Superior General of her order and put another nun in her place. They warned her a great deal about me, from what I could gather during our initial contact, but she was a good person who feared God and had some scruples. She let one of my servants know that if they thought she had even the least amount of esteem for me, or that I was content, they would not let her stay more than three days. Shortly after that, she told my servant that out of obedience she would have to do things that displeased me but she would not say what it was. But, later on, I found out that they were going to take one of my servants away from me.

On Assumption Day [August 15th] the priest from Saint-Sulpice came to hear our confessions and "Family" was the first to go. He told her that she had to leave and that they wanted to put other girls there to take care of me. He said he would take her back to her parents' house. She answered him that she had no parents and she was so distressed that she could not say anything else to him. She came to find me more dead than alive to tell me this.

Then, I went to confess and the priest told me that I was allowed to take communion the following day. Before leaving, he spoke to me of subjects that they had used to mistreat me and he insulted me saying, *"Well, now! Doesn't your patience ever end?"* All of this was to let me know that I only had to prepare myself for other things than what I had experienced up to this point. I answered him, *"No, sir, and they will become exhausted from persecuting me before I have had enough of suffering."*[8]

Their taking away my servants caused me great sorrow. I feared that it was because they wanted to turn me over to those whom they could control and who would say anything that seemed good to them; that would allow them to gain favor in their sight. It was a great peace of mind for me to be able to count on those servants that I had who were neither traitors nor spies. They did not make me worry in the least about every word I might say and they did not make sinister interpretations of the most innocent things I could do.

I dreamed again during that time about things that made a very strong impression on me. It seemed to me that I saw M. Pirot,[9] who made me feel very cold. I told him that I was very angry that they had treated me so poorly because of him. And although I had always noticed that he made an effort to keep me in Vincennes, nevertheless, I did not complain about him. And I bore witness to that fact to La Chétardie the first time they sent me there. My worry was that he, M. Pirot, might believe that I was not happy with him. He did not deny that keeping me in Vincennes was his plan, but he said that regardless of this, I was better off in his hands than in La Chétardie's. I asked why the archbishop of Paris was so irritated with me. He answered me that he was not as angry as La Chétardie pushed him to be.[10] And he added: *"Hide yourself and I will call him."*

Then, M. Pirot made him come and said to him: *"Well, now, sir, how are you pleased with Madame Guyon?"* and he called me by name. The other priest answered, with a gesture and manners that could only express the following: *"Worse than I can say."* And I saw that these gestures and manners led them to believe even worse things of me than he had ever said.

I told him, as I left the place where I was: *"I am a witness for you in the judgment of God. It is before that fearsome Judge that I refer you and from Him I demand justice for your malice."* While I was talking to him, it seemed to me that his priestly habit changed into course rags of dirty linen. Someone said to me: *"Leave this place, for you are in the worst hands you could ever be in."*

A while later, that sister, the good person, who had came to replace the troublesome one, came to tell me, all bathed in tears, that she was leaving. She had only done what she had to do out of obedience because they had ordered her to do it. She had honor and a conscience and I would see proof of this. If she had wanted to betray one person or another, she would not be leaving. I told her that the worst was over and since I was used to her, I begged her to stay. She answered that I did not know everything, for the worst had not happened yet and she saw horrible things to come. As for her, she did not expect riches and she did not want to do harm to her conscience. All this was said with the embarrassment of a person who had made a bad move, the consequences for which she had not foreseen. She was now tormented because of her scruples. Finally, she told me that she was going away, so that she could let the storm pass. Maddening things would come to pass, but she would have no part in them, and she urged me strongly to be patient. She admitted to me that they had made her sign statements that she knew nothing about but that she knew would be to my disadvantage.

I understood by her words that they had a plan to push me to all sorts of extremes and that they would use anything that their ingenuity could manufacture to get what they wanted, even though there was no proof or any reason for it. I understood quite well just why they brought so many resources into play and why they used so many machinations to make me appear guilty and publicize me as a person capable of the greatest crimes. But I could not imagine that they could impose darkness and injustice to the point of authorizing visibly false slander, and this was done by acts not only recognized as false, but fabricated and suggested by people supposedly of good character. I admit that I was not able to believe that the malice of men could ever go to such an excess, if the words that the priest from Saint-Sulpice told me here and there, in spite of himself, led me to the conclusion that there was nothing that one should fear when a great interest or great passion compels us. Nevertheless, despite the threats that they made, I remained at peace, ready for anything and nothing, in my God's will. If this persecution had only concerned me alone, I would have suffered quite a bit less. But, it had arisen in order to entrap persons of distinguished merit that they wished to oppress by linking them to a person [such as myself] so discredited.[11] I suffered extremely over the anguish of being the instrument or the pretext of persecution that they waged against them.[12] I sometimes said: "*O my God, let everything fall down on me. Let me be the scapegoat to expiate the errors of Your people. But spare the good and do not allow Your saints to become fodder for the birds of the heavens and the beasts of the fields.*"[13] You know, O my God, those who were acting for reasons of bitter zeal and completely human views, those who follow the torrent that they could not resist that pulled them along despite themselves, and finally You know those who, to please them, became masters of their passions or their weaknesses.[14] But You do not know any less those who become victims for Your truth and who, so as not to betray that truth, have sacrificed everything for it.[15]

The eve of all Saints Day, the priest from Saint-Sulpice came to confess me and told me that there was a person of very high standing who had provided a certificate in which I was convicted of horrible things for which he was a witness.[16] I then told him that he should come to see me or I should go to see him. This meeting could not take place where I was. If they wanted to tell me what it was about, it would not be very difficult to reveal the falsehood. He then told me again that it was also about my faith and that all the papers I had signed were not sincere. I asked him what proof there was about this and who else other than he could be informed of my sentiments, for he was the only person I had seen since I left Vincennes.

Sometime before that, he made the women who guarded me understand that I was a heretic and that it was because of a real excommunication that they had retracted communion from me. He forbade them to have a priest come if any illness came upon me suddenly such as an apoplexy or something else of that sort. It would be better to let me die without the sacraments because they had recently discovered horrible things against me. When he spoke to me, he led me to understand that it was about ancient crimes of mine. When he spoke to other people, it was about recent ones. They did not let that sister, of whom I have just spoken, stay for more than two months. They did not find her adequate to the purpose they had in mind and they had another sister come from the diocese of Chartres, who regarded me as a demon.

The priest from Saint-Sulpice brought me a Pastoral Instruction from the archbishop of Paris, to which he led me to understand I ought to subscribe. Since the Instruction was long, I asked him for some time to be able to read it. It was not difficult for me to see what his intention was in having me subscribe to what he asked me to do. That Instruction was full of turns of phrase and interpretations so contrary to the sentiments that I have had all my life that I would have subscribed to the most horrible death rather than accept a charge so contrary to the purity of my faith.[17] I let him know in no uncertain terms that I would never comply with such a thing and that he should desist in forcing me to. He told me that I should at least write a letter to the archbishop of Paris who had ordered him to make me read this Pastoral Letter, in which I had such a part. I told him that I would do it gladly and I sent him the following letter a few days later in these terms:

> Monsignor, I read the Pastoral Letter, with all respect and submission possible, that your Lord Bishop had sent to me through the priest from Saint-Sulpice. There are two things, Monsignor. The first concerns what my ignorance, disdain, lack of intelligence, and the little knowledge of the meaning of terms and their consequences caused me to place in my books; this did not explain why anyone could attribute deceit to them. And this is what I submit, Monsignor, as I already have and for which I have already given all the testimony possible, as a true Catholic, not only in submission to the Church and to the Sovereign Pontiff, but also to you, Monsignor, with all the sincerity and humility that a Christian heart is capable of. I have no other particular sentiment than that and no others than those for the entire Church.
>
> The other article of the letter, Monsignor, concerns the sentiment that your Lord Bishop attributes to me. I wish to believe that my ignorance and my poor expressions have caused your Lord Bishop to extract consequences so removed from the sentiments that I have always had by the grace of God. Nevertheless, I should express a very profound respect for your Lord Bishop and protest to you even in the presence of Our Lord Jesus Christ who knows that I do not lie. I have never had such sentiments, I do not have them now, and I will never have them, if it pleases God. I even have extreme horror towards them, and so I have always protested to your Lord Bishop and to all those who questioned me about the explanation for my faith. I have always been ready to shed my own blood for all the truths that the Catholic, Apostolic and Roman Church teaches.
>
> After having declared my sentiments so many times, I am very unhappy that no one can know, except for me, about the behavior that they attribute to me, but that I nevertheless have always given assurances that I do not indulge in. Despite my good will, I still have very much the correctness of my intentions, the sincere desire to belong to God, and to do everything for His glory. I still have, I repeat, written in

terms that make them attribute sentiments to me so contrary to those I have always held.

Regarding my prayers, I have tried to say them the best that I could in order to please God, but since it is not up to me to judge what is best and what is most useful, I have asked the priest [from Saint Sulpice] several times to confess me on your orders and do this confession as he deems appropriate. I renew that offer, Monsignor, to you personally and I assure your Lord Bishop that I am and will always be ready to pray as you order, according to my ability. I submit all my soul, my weak understanding and the tender sentiments of my heart to your obedience. I would prefer not to pray at all than to pray against what you command me to do. I believe that a prayer according to one's own volition would not please God in the least. Since I do not desire anything else than to please Him and do His holy will, I am indifferent to the choice of ways to pray. I will submit them to your Lord Bishop with all my heart. I do this, Monsignor, out of duty and inclination, with all due respect and submission, etc.

December 1697

The priest from Saint-Sulpice, after having read my letter, informed me that it was fine. He was not at liberty to justify this idea with the treatment that I had received. Instead, he assured me that he was working to have me released to my son's house. Then on the other hand, he assured the sisters that I would die in their house. One of them took me into her confidence. Such bad treatment and continual harassment made me exceedingly sad at times, but I never let on that I was distressed. And I even reproached myself for that sadness as unworthy of the sacrifice that I had done so many times for God with all my being, and for the love that he had given me on the cross.[18]

I went for a considerable time without seeing the priest from Saint-Sulpice, for I did not know what to attribute this absence to. He came at last and treated me with a great deal of fairness. He told me that the archbishop of Paris had been very pleased with my letter and he assured me of his consideration. Experience, however, had taught me more than once that if he acted nicely, that was exactly the moment when I had the most to fear, for he would begin fabricating more things against me. He ordered that they should allow me to have communion on Sundays and all the feast days, all this after denying me the Eucharist for three months. These highs and lows were very suspicious to me and I waited calmly for what Providence would bring from them.

During that time, they brought in a book for me to see that tore me apart in a strange way. A religious man of merit,[19] friend of a prelate who had a good opinion of me, wrote it, but he later changed his mind for reasons that I had spoken about earlier. The good religious man, forewarned by stories of all sorts that they leveled against me, and even more so by the words of that prelate, his friend, whom he reported to, thought he was rendering a service to God and to the Church in publicizing ideas about me that he had assumed. I hope that God will take into account his good intentions.[20]

But without entering into refutations of things that he reported, the truth is that Father La Combe did not stay with me in Grenoble.[21] He came there twice in twenty-four hours on behalf of Monsignor the bishop of Verceil in order to propose that I go see him. I was in Lyon for only a little while, about twelve days at the home of Madame Belof, a woman of merit, known by the entire city for her virtue and piety. She lived with Monsieur Thomé, her father, where I saw almost no one. And I never dressed in public. With similar things, they are able to force ideas on people who have not met me at any time or who have never seen me.

All the rest of the story from that good religious man is not true either, since they never ordered me to leave the diocese and the bishop of Grenoble himself begged me to set up housekeeping in Grenoble. I never saw a fifty-year-old nun in Lyon, or of any other age, and never met any nun there. The bishop of Geneva told me himself what Father La Combe had said to him on God's behalf (for this is how he expressed it) two or three years before I went to his diocese. In telling me this, he said to me: "*I felt that he was telling me the truth and he told me things that only God and I know.*" This did not stop him from assigning Father La Combe to me as Director, when he hired me to establish the New Catholics school in Gex. I have already spoken of this earlier.[22]

When they put me in Saint Mary's, they told Monsieur l'Official that I always wore clothes loosely and that they even saw into the hollow of my stomach. When he saw me dressed, as I am always and I have always been since my youth, he was so surprised that he could not stop himself from telling me so, and he also told Mother Eugénie.[23]

I also noted what helped me leave Verceil and the friendship that prelate had for me. The nun with whom that good religious man still said I had dealings, who is considered a saint in the order of Saint Ursula and is called Mother Good, was dead one year earlier before my arrival in that region. She has written some things, to tell the truth, but they are all brought to light.

I do not understand how that good religious man, so respected elsewhere, could have decided to attribute such weaknesses of mine concerning vague and uncertain relationships, unless he thought he had rendered glory to God in discrediting a person that they believed so dangerous and so capable of doing harm. I only plead that they pay attention to persons that they have regarded as friends during all the stages of my life, whom I have seen and with whom I have interacted on familiar terms. It will be easy to judge the foundations that they used to spread so much falsehood and so much calumny.

I omit many very important things in order to be brief, only writing even this because of my weakness. I only write a half a page sometimes in one day and I only write the pure truth, along with a great deal of reluctance.[24] And far from growing, my wealth is diminishing. I believe that without the trial that they had in Rome, they would not have tormented me so much.[25]

New Trials in Vaugirard

As was told to me later, when these matters were ended, the more they made me hateful, the more they charged me with disgrace and infamy, and the more they believed that, to speak more correctly, the more they deluded themselves in dazzling the public about this lofty, violent process with which they pushed that investigation that had been taken to Rome from the beginning. And they attempted to make part of this indignation, leveled against me, fall on the bishop of Cambrai because he had appeared to hold me in esteem and they thought that he was one of my friends.

A portly peasant girl who served as a maid to that sister who guarded me, and had no interest at all in persecuting me, was shocked to see all that they did to me and she could not prevent herself from saying so to her confessor, who began to hold me in esteem because of all of that. And from then on, I received all the assistance that he could give. Since many poor people came to that house, I had them receive alms through the help of that sister who, in the expense books that she kept, put so much down for charity. The priest from Saint-Sulpice found out about it and forbade her to write these things down in her expense book and he told her that it should not appear that I had done anything good.[26] Those alms for the poor were jotted down as other expenses and I agreed that the alms that I had should go to the sisters, but many people did not believe this. Many injured people came to get treatment from the sisters, but they barely attended to them. They asked me to do it, and I cured them.[27]

NOTES

1. Guyon repeatedly requested that her case be turned over to the secular authorities. She believed that she would find justice from state officials rather than church officials.

2. One of the members of Parliament helped publish her book *A Short and Easy Method of Prayer*. Gondal cites a Monsieur Giraud, a counselor of Parliament (*Madame Guyon* 283). See John J. Hurt, *Louis XIV and the Parlements: The Assertion of Royal Authority*, Manchester and New York: Manchester University Press, 2002, for a discussion of the *parlements* of France (Note the French spelling used here). The Conciergerie, located on the Île de la Cité, represents secular government, not ecclesiastical courts. Presumably some sort of due process was possible there.

3. The Fénelon affair involved his defense of mysticism with the publication of the *Maxims of the Saints* in 1697. Bossuet retaliates with his *Relation sur le quiétisme* [*Report on Quietism*]. King Louis, Bishop Bossuet, and Archbishop Fénelon all requested the intervention of the Pope in the Great Conflict. King Louis XIV exiled Fénelon from court on August 3rd, 1697.

4. The liquid measures or casks are about 100 to 140 liters and the écu equals 3 to 5 francs or one dollar (Gondal *Récits* 82 n3). Prisoners were expected to pay for their own food and drink (Gelfand, *Imagination in Confinement: Women's Writings from French Prisons* 65).

5. This poisoning provides more evidence that some in this community believed that Guyon was a witch, i.e. they wished that she would die in order to end any possible curse on the community. That is a common way they would treat witches in the 1600s. For reference, see Marie A. Conn, *Noble Daughters: Unheralded Women in Western Christianity, 13th to 18th Centuries*, Connecticut: Greenwood Press, 2000.

6. This is evidence that Bossuet was involved because he had written in his document that she should face the fire or scaffold, i.e. be executed.

7. This is a reference in scripture to Proverbs 15:3. "The eyes of the Lord are in every place, keeping watch on the evil and the good."

8. This line reflects a major theme in Guyon's theology. In suffering the believer becomes united to God and hence the believer enjoys the resources and strength of God. When suffering ceased, Guyon prayed for more suffering, as did Teresa of Avila.

9. Doctor Pirot, also known as L'abbé (abbot) Pirot, was named as Guyon's confessor during her imprisonment. See Loskoutoff, 151.

10. Guyon believed that God revealed reality to her though her dreams. Hence, she understood that La Chértadie was misrepresenting the Archbishop of Paris to her.

11. These events also implicated Guyon's friends, such as the Duke of Beauvillier (Gondal *Récits* 88 n12).

12. Guyon did not wish to harm Archbishop Fénelon's ministry. She believed in the importance of his work for the future of France.

13. The term scapegoat means the object on which the sins of Israel are projected and then driven out of the community. The reference for this is Leviticus 16:6-11. Guyon was being driven out of the community, though like the goat, she did not deserve this. She continues in her prayer to quote the prophet Isaiah who warns that the Israelites will be eaten by the beasts of the field because the leaders of Israel are asleep and not warning the Israelites of danger. The scriptural reference for this is reference is Isaiah 56:10. In essence, Guyon is praying for wisdom of the human leaders who are passing judgment on her.

14. Guyon in her book *Spiritual Torrents* encourages believers to let themselves be carried by their abandonment to God that is like an inner torrent. In this passage, she uses the same metaphor of torrent for those acting opposed to God.

15. Here Guyon refers to what she names the martyrdom of the Holy Spirit, i.e. that the Holy Spirit annihilates those willing to be a testimony for God.

16. Gondal cites this letter as probably from the bishop of Grenoble, Cardinal Le Camus, who wrote to the bishop of Chartres that Madame Guyon influenced a young woman, Cateau Barbe, while in the Savoie region. Guyon writes about this in her *Autobiography*, Vol. 2, 73-81. The woman accused Madame Guyon of being a "sorceress" pg. 74. Tronson also picks up this event and reports it, without verifying its authenticity (*Récits* 89 n13). See also Gondal (*Madame Guyon* 164 n6).

17. In Guyon's theology, her previous dream about the Archbishop of Paris would have prepared for the blow of this critical letter. Her dream encouraged her to believe that he was not as angry as the priest represented him. The Archbishop of Paris was appointed to this much desired position partially because Madame de Maintenon wanted him to have this power. His criticism of Guyon could have been a test of her to see how she would respond. That she was eventually released provides some evidence that her reply satisfied his questioning of her.

18. In her theology Guyon emphasizes both the sacrifice of Jesus and the sacrifices that every Christian is called to make.

19. Gondal cites the *Life of Mgr Jean d'Arenthon d'Alex, Bishop of Geneva* published in 1697 by Innocent Le Masson, superior general of the Chartreux. This biography contains unsubstantiated accusations against Mme Guyon (*Récits* Gondal 94 n18). Guyon writes in her *Autobiography* that while in Geneva, she confronted one of d'Arenthon's staff, a man called the Little Bishop, who was sexually harassing a beautiful nun. Madame Guyon also talked to the Bishop of Geneva about this incident.

20. In the following two paragraphs, Guyon addresses particular accusations made against her about the time when she was traveling around Europe from 1681-1685.

21. Madame Guyon writes about her work and ministry in Grenoble in her *Autobiography*, Vol. 2, 65-81.

22. Madame Guyon discusses these events in the Savoie region in the second part of her autobiography. (Gondal *Récits* 95 n20).

23. Mother Eugénie was the superior of the convent of the Visitation of Saint Mary in Paris where Mme Guyon was first interrogated about her writings (Gondal *Récits* 95 n21).

24. In her *Short and Easy Method of Prayer*, Guyon discusses that she wrote this treatise very quickly. Her prison memoirs are difficult for her. She expresses many times that she does not want to defend herself but against so many inaccuracies in this book, she feels she needs to speak out against this. Her dilemma is whether to allow God alone to defend her or whether she should speak out herself.

25. In 1697 the trial was beginning amidst very heated debate in Rome. This would have made Madame Guyon's situation very important to many powerful leaders, including Louis XIV, Bishop Bossuet, and Pope Innocent XII. This same year Miguel de Molinos died in Rome with many believing that the Vatican executed him.

26. Because Louis XIV wished the condemnation of Fénelon's book, the priest wished to help Louis by making Guyon appear as a witch. In this way, they hoped that a condemnation of Guyon would help achieve a condemnation of Fénelon.

27. Throughout her ministry, Guyon made medicines for the sick. This could have intensified the idea that she was a witch because of the common perception that witches made potions.

Chapter Four

The Letter from the Priest of Saint-Sulpice

Madame Guyon includes the full text of the letter dated May 1698 written to her by her confessor and interrogator La Chétardie who accuses her of being a hypocrite and a liar. He claims that she lives extravagantly, demands the best wines and meats while telling her followers, especially impressionable young noblewomen, that she shuns the pleasures of this world. He will no longer be her confessor and berates her writings, especially her treatise on prayer and her autobiography as proof of her heresy. An interesting detail of her defiance of him is her use of the words of Seneca that she wrote on a door in the convent gardens, "The coward seeks fortune and the unhappy man is worthy of respect." The priest from Saint-Sulpice interprets this statement as a refusal to repent. If this letter is authentic, Madame Guyon uses it to show just how seriously she had to take matters, for any request or action on her part in her confinement leads to further interrogations.

After having spent about twenty months in that house, where I suffered all that one can imagine, I received a long letter from the priest of Saint-Sulpice[1] and I found a way to send it to a person of confidence to keep it for me. Since it was written with much bitterness and gall, one may be surprised that all the crimes, old and new, that they spoke to me about every moment and for which the evidence, they said, was so clear and certain. They publicized this evidence with such talent and care, yet finally those crimes, as I was saying, only amounted to reading newspapers of all sorts, reading fairy tales, they called novels, eating green peas, drinking wine from Alicante, having a little dog and a parrot, and other things of that sort that may be seen in this letter. I wish to include this letter here so that the things that they have accused me of are not trivialized.

What is difficult to imagine or even more difficult to understand is that in this same letter, he [La Chétardie] assures me that he is bringing justice to me in believing that I am quite distanced from the unfortunate maxims that they attribute to the Quietists,[2] maxims that have been none the less the foundation of so many persecutions that I was forced to endure for fifteen or sixteen years and with which they used to discredit me as the lowest of all creatures. Here is the letter:

Madame,

Here is a letter that is going to surprise you, but I cannot hide the sorrow that your conduct has caused me. The just reasons I believe to have regarding this matter have increased so much and seemed so considerable that there is no way to sustain them any more than to explain myself to you. The zeal that I should have for your salvation, and the obligation that I have to respond to the confidence that Monsignor the archbishop of Paris has shown to me in entrusting you to my care, the interests of the Church, and several other important reasons have obliged me to open my heart to you, since you do not open yours to me, to tell you the truth that I believed I would betray if I kept silent any longer. God who sees the deepest intentions is my witness that I only come here to satisfy my conscience, which presses on me; I do not come to attract reproach from the righteous Judge who makes me render an exact account of the enlightenment and progress that He gives for the guidance of souls for whom one is in charge. I have even withdrawn myself from you more than usual for the past few months since I could not resolve the problem of administering the sacraments to you, given the state of blindness and false peace that you seemed to be in.

Here is, Madame, what gives me great concern in your regard, and what should not cause you any less concern either. I urge you to reflect calmly and seriously before God on the thing in the world that is most important to you and on which for us is the last consequence for our not being deceived. Once more, I declare to you that only charity and the pure desire to be useful to you have opened my mouth, and do not open it such as I am, but only after many prayers and requests repeated to God to not allow me to trouble you negatively about this. Neither should I say anything to you in His Spirit. I imagine that I will perhaps be exonerated, because I give testimony to myself that no one else in the world, or no other human view forces me to act in this situation.

First of all, Madame, how does true and solid pity relate to the spirit of presumptuousness and esteem of oneself? You have told me, among other things, in conversation and precise words, that since your youth, although you were very beautiful, you always lived in innocence. You had won souls for God, especially those of young women of nobility in the Court, which had attracted the indignation of many people against you.[3] Your books had converted many people. You were a servant of God. You were dear to God. And in mistreating you, we mistreated God

You even wrote to me, I believe. And if I had not stopped you from these dangerous attitudes, on orders of Monsignor the archbishop himself who charged me to do so, I fear that you would have added others to the list. As for the rest, they dealt with you harshly and made you suffer what you had to endure. If they had cut off your head at least you would have died a martyr, if I am not wrong, and you said that this was done for the truth.

In my presence at Vincennes, you allowed your chambermaid to say to you arrogantly and presumptuously, more than once, that I saw in you the most saintly person on earth that there was. It was necessary that the Monsignor the archbishop not have compassion for your suffering but they should have compassion for him, since he was persecuting such a great saint as you for no reason.[4] It is true that you laughingly told her to go away.

What shall I say about your moments of anger and indignation, not to mention your outbursts, so great and so frequent ever since I had the honor of knowing you? In all truth it was difficult to believe that charade. I am able to say that I had scarcely ever seen livelier outbursts in the rashest and most passionate of worldly people! How many times was I forced to keep quiet, hide, or even suppress many things so as not to irritate you! You told me, in one of your tirades, that you wanted to present your case to the king so that they would bring you to trial to determine your innocence or guilt. But you did not want to be judged by priests or Church officials because they did not have the integrity or good faith that one sees in the laity.[5] You also objected to representatives and insisted on being tried by Parliament. Once, you wrote two letters to me in an ostensible passionate rage. You even showed those letters, as I found out later, to the nuns that you were staying with and they urged you to get rid of them, all to no avail. You insisted on following your own whims instead of taking their good advice. You put in one of those letters, among other things, that if I did not do what you asked me to do, you would pray to God to let you know that you belonged to Him and that I mistreated God in mistreating you and that He should not pardon me for that. Who ever made prayers like that to God? And when a penitent speaks to her confessor in such a manner, how then can he ever be of any use to her?

When they wanted to block up a window and a door behind your apartment, something you yourself had expressed a desire to do, what fire, what indignation did you not demonstrate? You opposed the entire project with such force, you and your chambermaids, that it was necessary to postpone the whole thing and give in, until you calmed down. They waited until you became calm and capable of listening to reason. As for the nuns who had charge of you, they did not want to allow you to be able to look out the window of their apartment that borders the street where at that time there were a lot of people. But you and your servants, how did you treat them? Let us not discuss the insulting words that you hurled at them, although they assured you that they would not use that sort of language because your superiors had ordered it that way. However, what is even more shocking is that you added that you had been in a convent where, even though the bishop of the place had forbidden the nuns to give you certain things, they did not let you have them, but you got them anyway, despite the prohibition of them. In truth, Madame, are these the words and maxims of a soul who sets herself up as a director of spiritual life and undertakes to teach others the *Short and Easy Method to Attain the Highest Perfection in the Least Amount of Time?*[6]

What would your blindness lead to after that, Madame, if you did not become the least bit suspect yourself and if you still mistook yourself for a prophetess?[7] You know the consequences, Madame, and the matter is too important and too appropriate for you to open your eyes and overlook it here, despite the trouble it causes you. In August 1696, you told me positively, during two visits I paid you, both in the space of eight days, and this was at Vincennes where you had no human way of learning what was happening in the world: you assured me, as I was saying, that you had two kinds of visions or revelations, call them what you will. In these visions, you found out that we were on the brink of great revolutions and that the king was going to die soon. You warned that Madame de Maintenon, M. de Beauvillier, and M. the archbishop of Cambrai [Fénelon] should know about this and there was not a moment to lose, since it was a matter of the salvation of the king's soul. You insisted on writing to the archbishop of Cambrai. You gave me a letter to take to him immediately. You insisted that I tell him this important secret in person, his being a person of consequence. You assured me that when you had this sort of revelation time after time, at least twice, it was a sign of their authenticity. However, Madame, it was all a delusion. The month of September came and went. The king, thank heaven, was well and you should have turned red with shame.

And then when I insisted on using this wonderful prediction, so positive, so pressing and so well written, to challenge you regarding your understanding and your own mind, how you appeared embarrassed and upset! Nevertheless, you imagined that you could muster some sort of response in this uncertain future and by chance you muttered that the month of September of 1697 had not yet passed. What a pity! Well, it is now over and it has been over for quite a while and there is nothing to respond to you with other than the menacing words of Scripture regarding false prophets.[8] For, this is not the only false prophecy you have made, as your best friends have confirmed. *One can be assured that it is not the Lord who speaks through him, but the depravation of an arrogant heart that had seduced him. This is why you should not fear all these vain prophecies.*[9]

But, Madame, what to say about the story of your *Life* that you have written, so full of fanciful visions that you yourself could never sustain after reading them? Not even your best friends, or anyone else for that matter, are able to read them without confusion or indignation. You have even dared to write several Commentaries on Scripture, certainly full of errors.[10] You are still poised and ready to condemn them with the same facility you wrote them, or so you contend. Have you not maintained incessantly that no one can find anything bad in your works except for a few terms and expressions that your judgment concealed the meaning and importance of? However, as for the rest, you found your doctrine in the books of the greatest saints of the Church and you are ready to justify yourself.[11] You claim you had no retraction to make other than a few words here and there and that one must not speak to you of anything more about this. These are your own terms, written down the very day in which you uttered them in a highly emotional state.

I admit that after all of that, you had subscribed to a rather formal disavowal of your errors. But, in good faith, Madame, are you deeply convinced of having written them? Do you truly detest your errors? Do you regret having spread dangerous maxims that have done dreadful harm to people who believed you too easily? Do you regret causing in great part the distressing division that troubles the Church at the present time?[12] Not at all! You give no sign of repentance and many times you have testified with great tranquility that you had no scruples for anything and that you were the same as you were before. All that has happened according to you is considered as null and void. You are still a persecuted saint as your two chambermaids scream incessantly. There is nothing to censure in your conduct nor is there anything in need of rewriting in your books other than a few terms whose meaning you did not know.

But, Madame, who will ever believe that a person such as yourself, who speaks the mother tongue so well and who claims to be so knowledgeable of mystical theology, could be so ignorant of what these French words of devotion mean?[13] Is this better to dismiss your errors than to hide them under a beautiful, yet unrefined ignorance? If you are as ignorant as all that, as you aver, why do you meddle in dogmatizing, teaching, and publishing new doctrines in the Church? You see your way clear to causing so many scandals there! What do you not keep silent about in accordance with the commandment of the Apostle Paul,[14] in order to learn orthodox doctrine, in which you were not well enough informed to speak of correctly, especially as a teacher, since you did too much teaching?

By the same token, Madame, where did you dredge up that sublime theology that the most enlightened saints have taught us and in whose works you boast of having found your doctrine? Who would be surprised to learn that after almost two years you never asked me for a book of devotion? Who would believe that a soul that claims to be elevated to such high perfection, united with God by a love so pure, favored by the gift of contemplation and prophetic visions, had read news of the entire world for more than a year: the gazettes of France, Flanders, Holland, the newspapers of the Scholars[15], the Gallant Mercury, Aesop's fables in verse, novels full of amorous intrigue for which the title alone would scandalize not only devout people but even those mediocre or modest sages? How was it, Madame, that you had no scruples at all in keeping books and news for such a long time? You sent for them regularly and you filled your head with them and read them so avidly that even the time of Lent and the eve of Palm Sunday were not enough to stop your delving into them. We allowed your excesses because we wanted to see just where your unruliness would lead, all of this so as to make you come back to yourself and make you feel that you are other than what you believe.

What would they say then, Madame, if they knew about your life? You are so little chagrined by this behavior and so subject to the satisfaction of the senses that there would be no semblance of allowing frequent participation in the sacraments to someone who lived in that way. How much trouble we had in finding a rather good wine for you in all of Paris! The wine that cost twenty cents a pint was not up to your standards and your stomach suffered as a result, or so you said. It was necessary to purchase a half-barrel for forty or fifty écus, and buy it at a local tavern in large amounts. Who would not be a bit shocked to learn that you imbibed fashionable liqueurs, wine from Alicante, or even from Spain? You even smoked tobacco in lavish quantity and the last box they sent you cost nine francs! Who would think that a person so dead to the pleasures of this earth would take care to raise and find the best poultry, eat the best meat from the butcher shop and the best fish, have the best first fruits in season, asparagus, green peas, or artichokes? You spend whole days in the garden in summer and boiled pots and cooked your soup there. By chance, as they learned, you set fire to the wooden molding of the house where you live. You amuse yourself with linnets, turtledoves, dogs and parrots and other silliness. You found a way, in the condition you are in, to bet or have someone else place the bet, on the lottery in Paris, where you falsified your name as "The Unhappy One," and you won some pictures; they were so disreputable that it was necessary to exchange them for other things, as you told me you had ordered to be done. I only condescend to invoke such detail, Madame, out of necessity and in spite of myself. My only motivation is a desire to make you understand that you are not the person you think you are or that you have led other people to think you are.

And although these trifles are not criminal offenses in themselves, since some amusement is allowed, especially for a lady of your station, wealth, and age, your health requires some attention. However, Madame, when they allow you some entertainment, you should not set yourself up as an extraordinary person or delude yourself into thinking you are of sublime perfection. You should come down from that lofty sphere and join the ranks of the simple faithful who march along the common way and who adhere to the observation of precepts. [16] You should not set yourself up as the teacher of spiritual life who has found the "short and easy method" to display the highest sanctity possible.[17] This is what you had set yourself up to be, Madame. *For if one wishes to suspect that you are beginning to be in error regarding those people who maintain that in giving their soul to God once, they are able to offend true piety or satisfy their sensuality, may it only please God, Madame, that I have these thoughts of you*[18].

But I know well that those whom we honor as saints, in the very midst of their infirmities and very severe persecution, still led penitent, holy lives. They were always in prayer. They gave rare examples of patience and humility. They even would believe themselves lost, if during these times of trials and tribulation, they were allowed to experience a lessening of torment that they would not endure from anyone, whoever he might be, in a community so inconsistent and who without a doubt surprised and badly informed those from the inside and those from the outside.[19] The house where you have been in retreat was not able to grant a life similar to the high perfection that you claim to profess.[20] For you judge well, Madame, that all this could not be secret and that it was necessary for several people to serve your needs and to have knowledge of this, for things have passed through their hands before their eyes. And do not complain, Madame, that I speak too much of this. Do yourself justice and testify to yourself that I have suppressed many important items that I wished to spare you from.

In effect, it is with reason that I stop here, for I know the extreme pain that the reading of this letter will cause you, but I am aware also of the indispensable obligation that I have to write this to you. The doctor who spares his patient the salutary cure because it is bitter or painful, is cruel, and the doctor who gives that medicine to his patient is charitable. You know, Madame, how many times I told you that Providence had allowed you to be placed in solitude where you are now so that you may examine your conscience seriously and remedy it effectively. Your salvation was related to the good implementation of this sweet, comfortable retreat that fortunately was secured for you. They offered you all sorts of assistance for this. You gave a very exact account to God that this was the happiest time of your life. I discharged my conscience of this in saying to you that I could do nothing more for you.

All these methods, all this progress, were they very successful? You know they were, Madame. But in truth, I believe myself completely useless with respect to your welfare if you refuse to take more advantage of it and if you insist on remaining there. I implore you, Madame, to recognize yourself, humble yourself, confess the truth, share true feelings of repentance, confess your errors in good faith, and lament the scandal and division that you in large part caused in the Church. Without this, Madame, I would be a blind guide and I would answer to God for the lethargic deadening that I believe you to be immersed in.[21] I would ask permission from Monsignor the archbishop to find it good for me to withdraw and give you over to a man more enlightened than I, who has more influence over your spirit, for whom you have more consideration and for whom you suspect less as acting because of politics or human respect.

For, Madame, to whom do you wish to address these words that you wrote more than a year ago in bold letters on the door of the little grotto in your garden if it was not I? Here are those words: *"The coward seeks fortune and the unhappy man is worthy of respect"* (Seneca).[22] After that, how could a spiritual director be of any use to you? How could you have confidence in him? Besides, how to refrain from believing that you still consider yourself a poor, innocent persecuted one and that you suffer for justice? Consequently, you think you do not have to repent for anything, when one still reads the other words that you have written in capital letters compared to the ones you wrote before, with which you insisted without a doubt to designate as: "As they have persecuted me, they will persecute you and they will believe that they are rendering service to God in persecuting you" [Jesus Christ].[23]

Such is the idea that you have of yourself and the spirit of compunction that encourages you to continue. It is then appropriate, Madame, that since I cannot be of any good to you, I will withdraw at the good pleasure of Monsignor the archbishop. Nevertheless, I will not stop being, in accordance with God's wishes, in true charity, Madame, your very humble and very obedient servant.

J. de La Chétardie, rector of Saint-Sulpice[24]

The many reproaches in this letter and the shrewd twists of phrases used here did not tell me anything new about the hostility that the priest from Saint-Sulpice had against me, or about what he had used to influence the archbishop of Paris. I had known what I was up against for a long time. The continual illnesses that I had, the anxiety of such harsh captivity of the poor servant girls who served me with such great affection, but who needed some recreation at certain moments when the situation was at its limits: all of this could justify many things or excuse them, if one entered into some detail on the things that the letter accused me of doing. But I leave all that as extraneous to the issues arising after many years in prison and the eighty interrogations that they made me endure, most of them for eight to ten hours at a stretch.

I will only say in passing that it was the priest from Saint-Sulpice himself who pressed me several times to read the gazettes and he became angry with me if I refused to do it. The novels were fairy tales that he had brought me himself on behalf of my daughter. My servants enjoyed reading them sometimes as a diversion in their free time. Most of all, I read the history of the Church by Joseph,[25] and I had more than fifty books of devotion that we read almost constantly: the Bible, the New Testament, the Lives of Saints, etc.[26] We fasted on every Friday and Saturday of the year, during all of Lent and twelve days of Advent. But when a heart is set against something to a certain degree, the same things that could edify one become a subject of scandal, for an eye imprinted in one color only sees objects in that same color.

A nun who guarded me gave me that letter. They ordered her to observe me while I read it to see if I became terribly upset or if I simply got angry. I did not say a word to that girl and I dealt with her in my usual jovial manner. She began to cry and I consoled her. I assured her that I knew she had no evil designs because she had been ordered to spy on me.

She told me that she had a terrible interrogation session with the priest from Saint-Sulpice about me. He had asked her if I ever spoke about God with her and she answered that I did not. *"Admit then that she is ungodly,"* he told her. *"Sir,"* she answered him, *"Since I am cold blooded and she had a good fire going, I sometimes went to see her to warm up. They were reading the lives of saints in the room and we sometimes spoke of the circumstances of those lives." "So, she did speak to you about God then,"* he said. *"Yes, sir,"* answered the girl. *"That is all I wanted to know. She is proselytizing and that I all I wanted to know."* Anything that nun said even though it was only a form of conversation, she had to put in writing and sign it.

They also interrogated a peasant girl who answered rudely that she only knew good things about me. He told her that she was only a beast. And she told him that she did not have enough intelligence to see any evil there. He chased her out of his room with insults. She told her confessor about this and he ordered her to tell me about it.

They used the same method with the first nun who had tormented me so much and who was so devoted to them. They made her sign many things without reading them, half of them threats and the other half promises. As soon as she carried out these orders, they took her to the archbishop of Paris who made her the Superior General of her Congregation. I believe I have already mentioned this, for I am giving an account here of things, not as they happened in sequence but as they come to my mind or as I remembered them. That same nun nevertheless had not trampled so much on her own conscience that she did not have some terrible remorse left for what she had done. She came to me one day crying and told me that they made her sign many things against me without letting her read them first and that, if some misfortune happened to me and they produced her signature as proof, I should ask to confront her and she would say everything about what they had forced her to sign.

But they never spoke to me of any of these things during the interrogations that they did later, nor did they bring up anything else about it. They only wanted to bring this out in public without letting me know about it for fear that I would try to defend myself. Perhaps they wanted to secure for the future a justification of such violent and hateful conduct for which later on they could be held accountable. Only God knows.

The peasant girl told me one day that she went to the rooms of the priest of Saint-Sulpice. He let her stay there since he thought she was so stupid that he did not guard against her; he thought she was too ignorant to understand what was happening. There was a scribe there, that same forger of whom I will speak later on regarding further events in my life. That girl noticed very clearly that they were forging handwriting, for the priest from Saint-Sulpice told him, *"That letter is not right. He does not write an L the way you do."*[27] She told all of this to her confessor who ordered her to tell me about it.

NOTES

1. Joachim Trotti de La Chétardie (1636-1714), the priest from Saint-Sulpice, sent this letter dated May 1698 that Guyon copies into her autobiography. Its authenticity has not been confirmed, for the letter has not been found (Gondal *Récits*, 99 n1).

2. With the term maxims Guyon picks up the title of Fénelon's treatise on mysticism. Although she is not mentioned in this work, the *Maxims of the Saints* (1697) has been interpreted as a defense of Guyon's theology (James, *The Conflict Over the Heresy of "Pure Love" in Seventeenth Century France* 91-116).

3. Guyon was asked by Mme de Maintenon to teach in her school for disadvantaged girls of the nobility at Saint-Cyr (James, *The Pure Love* 13-15). She was later asked to stop her work by the Bishop of Chartres, Paul Godet. This expulsion caused many to distrust and criticize Guyon.

4. In Guyon's theology one is to have compassion for those who sin because of the serious ramifications of their behavior. In Christian theology sin creates problems both in this life and in eternity.

5. This comment reveals this priest's understanding of Guyon's respect for the laity. Guyon's theology influenced many Protestant denominations, particularly the Quakers, in her belief that the divine communicates not only through the church hierarchy but through the laity. This belief caused concern among the Catholic hierarchy.

6. This is the title of Guyon's treatise on prayer published in 1685. See Laude (98-142) for an edition of this work.

7. Bossuet compared Fénelon to a second century heretical prophet named Montanus and Guyon to Montanus' fellow prophet, Priscilla. Once again, the influence of Bossuet can be seen in this accusation.

8. The timing and accuracy of Guyon's prophecies are addressed in the document Supplement to the Life of Madame Guyon. Her followers believed that the timing of prophecies is never specifically known. The document quotes Guyon saying, "In respect of the time that these things will happen, these words have been impressed on me. We are not granted the knowledge of the time and the moment that God will reserve for his power." Some later believed that she could have been predicting the French Revolution. See *Pure Love*, pages 101-104.

9. This is a reference to Deuteronomy 18:22. "If a prophet speaks in the name of the Lord, but the thing does not take place or prove true, it is a word that the Lord has not spoken. The prophet has spoken it presumptuously; do not be frightened by it."

10. See Claude Morali's edition of Guyon's commentaries on the *Song of Songs* as an example of her Biblical commentaries.

11. The priest is referring to Guyon's book called *Justifications*.

12. This division, known as the Great Conflict, troubled relationships both in France and at the Vatican. Information about the Great Conflict had spread throughout Europe and the New World and created heated controversy.

13. Since childhood, Guyon had been known for her eloquence.

14. This reference to Paul that women keep silent in church (Gondal, *Récits* 107 n13) is frequently interpreted as a reason to keep women out of the pulpit as well.

15. Tronc edition ("Les prisons, récits autobiographique" 933 n74).

16. Guyon interpreted the *Song of Songs of Solomon* as instructing those who seek union with God to practice the "perpetual abandonment of every selfish interest" (39, translated James W. Metcalf, 1879). Because of that, they are to travel the common way of the church, which is to practice full participation in the sacraments and the community. At the same time, these persons practice the interior way of prayer. Because of her theology, she would have agreed with this priest's statement about going the common way. Possibly the priest knew this and was using this as a rhetorical device to gain her agreement on one point so that she would agree with his other ideas.

17. He is quoting the name of her most popular book, *The Short and Easy Method of Prayer*.

18. Gondal interprets this passage, underlined in the manuscript, as a kind of exoneration of Guyon (*Récits* 109 n14).

19. Perhaps this reference to community is an allusion to Guyon's "little church" that she discusses in Chapter one. By this she means her own congregation. However, it can also mean a kind of cabal of subversive activity. See Ulrike Krampl, "When Witches Became False."

20. Guyon believed that saints frequently had underdeveloped spiritual lives. The church felt comfortable with them and so named them as saints.

21. The priest is quoting from Matthew 15:14 and Matthew 23:24 by comparing himself to a blind Pharisee leading another blind person into disaster.

22. This is a reference to Lucius Annaeus Seneca (4 B.C.-A.D. 65), a Roman Stoic philosopher. According to theologian Charles Philip Price in *Principles of Christian Faith*, Stoic philosophy influenced the ethical standards in the New Testament letters. As such, Madame Guyon shows her understanding of the relationship between Stoicism and Christianity.

23. The reference is to John 15:20, "If they persecuted me, they will persecute you" (Gondal *Récits* 111 n15).

24. The zeal of this prosecuting priest can be understood in the context of Louis XIV's political campaign to rid France of any people who were not submissive Roman Catholic subjects. Louis aggressively sought judgment from the Pope against any Quietist. Louis revoked the Edict of Nantes to rid France of Protestants. He incarcerated Freethinkers in the Bastille. J. de La Chétardie sought approval from his superiors as part of this purge of many nonconforming French citizens.

25. This is probably a reference to Josephus, author of *Antiquities of the Jews* (c. 94 CE), which contains much of early Christian history.

26. *The Lives of the Saints* was written by the Archbishop of Genoa, Jacobus de Voragine, in the thirteenth century. Translated into French in the fifteenth

century, this religious book was very popular. The archbishop wrote at length about the important role of Mary in the history of redemption. Madame Guyon shared his belief about the ministry of Mary.

27. This could be a reference to the letter from Father La Combe that Guyon says is a forgery. The peasant girl overhears this conversation and the priest from Saint-Sulpice thought she was too simple-minded to understand that a forgery was in progress.

Chapter Five

The Letter from Father La Combe

Madame Guyon now receives a visit from the archbishop of Paris himself dressed in full regalia. He comes bearing a letter from her former confessor Father François La Combe now in prison, who admits to having taken inappropriate liberties with her. She is convinced that the letter is a forgery or forcibly written under threat of torture. Even her respectful demeanor in dealing with the archbishop is taken as a lack of humility and obedience. Every word she utters is distorted. A nun put in charge of her is promised a priorate if she can extract evidence to convict Madame Guyon. The judges in Rome, however, are indecisive in their examination of Fénelon, so if a conviction can be made regarding someone he has defended, then his case becomes clear. Thus, the relationship between the Barnabite Father La Combe and Madame Guyon now comes under scrutiny.

A few days after that long letter, the archbishop of Paris came to see me in full regalia.[1] He entered my cell with the priest from Saint-Sulpice, who was in despair because I had appeared to be so insensitive to his authority. He sat down and bade the priest to sit down next to him.[2] And since I was sitting in a spot that was against the sunlight, he had me placed in full light because he wanted to see me directly in front of him.

At first, he forced himself to speak sweetly to me and said: *"I have come to restore your relationship with the priest from Saint-Sulpice who complains about you very much; he does not want to serve as your confessor anymore."* I answered him: *"Monsignor, I do not believe I have given him any reason to complain about me and I have confessed with him out of obedience."*

That was all that needed to be said. For I was convinced, without deluding myself, that anyone else other than I would not have confessed to him, after having found out that this man had only worked to cause my downfall. But, as the priest from Saint-Sulpice dressed the part, I believed I was confessing to my dear Master [Jesus Christ] in confessing there. And I have always felt that he spoke to me so differently in the confessional than he did elsewhere; this confirmed for me the promise of Jesus Christ who often allows a bad priest to bless the person who confesses himself with a mean-spirited priest who makes him say what pleases him.[3] I do not judge him. I only point out the facts of this story that I would swear to by the Gospel.

To return to what I was saying, the archbishop of Paris told me: "But if he does not confess you, then no one else will want to do it!" "*Monsignor,*" I told him. "*The Jesuits would confess me if I were free.*" That response put him into a very bad mood.

He insisted on forcing me to make a public declaration that I had committed a large number of shameful licentious acts with Father La Combe; the archbishop of Paris made terrible threats to me if I did not declare that I had manipulated people of status and had deceived them, and that I was in a state of dissoluteness when I had written my books. At last, he displayed an anger that I had not expected of a man who had seemed so moderate to me in times past. He assured me that he would ruin me if I did not do what he wished.

I told him that I knew all about his prestige, for it must be noted that the priest from Saint-Sulpice had taken great care to inform me of his favor in telling me about the marriage of the archbishop's nephew [Adrien-Maurice de Noailles, Count of Ayen] with the niece of Madame de Maintenon [Françoise d'Aubigné].[4] The king had given him the royal shirt, which is only done for princes.[5] He had highly favored him in this marriage, and, in a word, this all could give me a great idea of the consideration this event provided for him in public. But God knows the case that I make for earthly fortunes. I answered him then that he could ruin me if he wished, and that only what pleased God would ever happen to me. Regarding that comment, he said to me: "*I would prefer to hear you say: 'I am in despair' than to hear you speak of God's will.*"

"But, Madame," said the priest from Saint-Sulpice to me, "*Admit that when you wrote your books, you were in a dissolute state*" "I would be lying to the Holy Spirit," I responded to him, "*if I confessed to such a falsehood.*" "We know what the Maillard woman said," replied the archbishop of Paris. (She is that glove maker of whom he had already spoken during the time when I was imprisoned in the convent of the nuns of Saint Mary). "*Sir, are you able to base your comments on a poor wretch who climbed over the walls of her cloister where she was a nun so that she could lead a life of excess for which they have witnesses, not to mention her theft? She finally got married and that is the rest of her horrid story.*" He told me: "She will go to heaven and you will go to hell. We have power to imprison and set free."[6] "But, sir," I replied to him, "*what do you want me to do? I only ask to satisfy you and I am ready for anything provided that I do not harm my conscience.*" He responded that he wanted me to confess that I had been dissolute during my entire life. If I did that, he would protect me and would say to everyone that I had converted. I made him see that it was impossible for me to find myself admitting to such a falsehood, and with that, he took a letter out of his pocket and he said that Father La Combe had written it.

The archbishop of Paris read it to me and then told me: "*You see that Father La Combe confesses to having taken liberties with you that could have been sinful.*" I was not embarrassed or surprised by that letter. As he approached me to consider it, I noticed that he concealed the address on it with care and even the handwriting appeared forged to me, although it bore some resemblance to his. I answered him that if Father La Combe had written that letter, either he must have been mad or the force of torture made him write it.[7] He told me: "*The letter is from him.*" – "*If the letter is from him,*" I told him, "*Then let me confront him with it, sir. That is a good way to discover the truth.*"[8]

The priest from Saint-Sulpice took over and made it be known that they would not pursue that tactic because Father La Combe only considered me a saint. They did not want to bring this affair to trial, but the priest would bring forth witnesses who would make me understand that they had convicted me.

The archbishop of Paris supported this idea, but I told him that if this happened, I would not say a word to him. He replied that they would make me talk a lot. "*No,*" I told him, "*They can make me endure what they want but nothing is capable of making me talk when I do not wish to do so.*"[9]

He told me that he was the one who got me out of Vincennes. I answered him that I had cried when I left there because I knew full well that they were removing me from one place in order to put me in another place where they could convict me of crimes. He told me that he knew full well that I had cried when I left Vincennes, but that it was my friends who had begged him to take charge of me; without those pleas they would have sent me very far away, to which I responded that they would have given me great pleasure in doing that.[10]

Then the archbishop of Paris told me that he was tired of me. I said to him: "*Sir, you could save yourself a lot of trouble if you wished. If it were not the profound respect that I have for you, I would tell you that I have my shepherd to whom you could hand me over.*"[11] He appeared embarrassed and he told me that he did not know what to do. If the priest from Saint-Sulpice did not want to be my confessor any more, he would not be able to find anyone else to take charge of me. He drew near me and said in a whisper, "*We will ruin you.*" I said in a loud voice, "*You have the power, sir. I am in your hands. You have all the prestige and I have only one life to lose.*" "*We do not want to take your life,*" he told me. "*You would believe yourself to be a martyr and your friends would believe it too. We must disabuse them of that.*"

Then, he swore to me, by the living God, as on the day of the last judgment, to say that I had never taken the least or even the slightest liberty with Father La Combe. I told him with all frankness and naiveté that cannot lie; when he [La Combe] arrived from a trip, for he had not seen me for a long time, he kissed me and took my head in his hands, which he did with extreme simplicity, and I did the same. Regarding these actions, he asked me if I had taken this to confession. I answered him that I had not and that I had not considered it a sin; the thought never even occurred to me. Father La Combe did not greet only me in that way, but all persons who were present whom he knew. *"Confess, then,"* said the priest from Saint-Sulpice, *"that you have lived in sin" "I will never say such a lie, sir,"* I replied to him, *"and what I told you has nothing to do with sin, for it is far from it."* If these are not the exact words, they at least convey the substance of my comments.

Since I spoke with a great deal of respect to the archbishop of Paris, he kept saying to me: *"Well, for God's sake, Madame, do not speak with such respect. Show more humility and obedience!"* There was another time when he let himself go to excess in his annoyance with me and said: *"I am your archbishop. I have the power to condemn you. Yes, I condemn you."* I responded to him smiling, *"Sir, I hope that God will be more indulgent and that he will not approve of that sentence."* He told me then that my servants would suffer martyrdom for my sake since I seduced everyone I came in contact with.[12] Another time, he demanded that I sign a paper saying that I had committed crimes and enormous sins. He attributed to me the humility of Saint Francis who had said these things about himself. When I told him that I would not do it, he accused me of pride and harshness. If I had confessed in the manner of Saint Francis, they would have publicized this as my recognition of having committed these vile deeds.

He asked me again if I were sure that grace was within me. I responded to this that no one knows if one is worthy of love or hate. He reproached me for the story of my *Life* and wanted to make me put in writing that the desire to make myself worthy of public acclaim had motivated me to write all the lies that my life story was full of.

He reproached me for having selected the best meat and examined the record the nun had kept regarding my food: poultry, wine, nothing was omitted. In truth, everything was written down there with emphasis and I remember an extensive entry in which there were chickens, pigeons, and capons at thirty-six sols. Wine costs were exaggerated as if I drank with excess. I often drank wine mixed with quinine tonic because of the fever that consumed me continually.[13] But, I did not open my mouth regarding any of this.

At last, after many continual angry threats that I should have expected, the archbishop of Paris left and the priest from Saint-Sulpice remained and told me : *"Here is a copy of the letter from Father La Combe. Read it carefully. Write to me about it and I will be at your service."* I did not answer him at all and the archbishop of Paris summoned the priest to come back. Here is a copy of that letter:

> It is before God, Madame, that I sincerely recognize that there were delusions, errors and sins in certain things that happened with too much freedom between the two of us. I regret and detest every maxim and all conduct that draw one away from the commandments of God and those of the Church. I highly disavow all that I was able to do or say against the sacred and inviolable laws and I urge you for the sake of Our Lord to do the same, so that you and I might make amends, as much as possible for us, for all the evil that is in us that may have set a

poor example for others. This includes all that we have written that can provide the slightest breach of the rules of conduct that the Holy Catholic Church professes to whose authority one should be subject, under the judgment of prelates, all doctrine of spirituality for whatever degree one claims to have. Once more I beseech you for the love of Jesus Christ that we have recourse to the only remedy through penitence. Only through a truly repentant and obedient life in every respect will we be able to efface the regrettable impressions we have caused in the Church by our false moves. Let us confess, you and I, our sins, humbly before heaven and earth and let us only be ashamed at having committed them, but let us not be ashamed at having confessed them. What I declare to you here proceeds from my complete candor and freedom. And I pray to God to inspire in you the same sentiments that I seem to have received from His grace and that I feel obliged to have.

Written on the 27 of April, 1698
Signed

Dom François de La Combe
Barnabite

When the archbishop of Paris read this letter to me, I asked to see it. He had a great deal of difficulty in doing this for me. Finally, he held it without wanting to place it in my hands, and I saw the handwriting. I concluded instantly that it was a forgery. I thought that it was a decisive blow for me to avoid pretending to see myself involved in a confrontation with Father La Combe while I was in prison.[14] This was another way to show the falsehood of these accusations. This is what led me to say simply that if the letter were from him, he must have gone mad in the sixteen years since I saw him or that the torture he endured made him say such things.

But after they left and I was able to read the copy that the priest from Saint-Sulpice had left me, I did not doubt that the letter was truly a forgery. That copy was not the original of his letter because they had corrected a "V" in a different way from those that Father La Combe would have written, and it was corrected by a hand that I recognized had served as a model for the scribe who forged the main corpus of writing in which the "V"s were neglected and bore no resemblance to Father La Combe's handwriting at all.

It is impossible for me to relate all that I thought after finishing that conversation. And it is certain that the respect that I believed I owed to a man of character prevented me from giving him an immediate denial to make him understand that I saw the deception in all its extensiveness and the shamefulness of the trap they had set for me. But I could not bring myself to embarrassing him to such an extent, other than allowing him to conclude that I believed the letter to be authentic. With this, I allowed them to boldly present that letter to the public, which would have given me grounds for revealing its falsehood to everyone and letting the public judge the entire piece by the sample.[15]

For what could be more natural to justify such violence and not allow people who esteemed me any room for esteem than to take me to trial on such evidence and with such witnesses so capable of disabusing them? The public so forewarned would have grasped at the slightest appearance, and my friends that I held so strongly in my heart, or so they said, turned away from their prejudices and would have nothing to reply; they ought to have been the first to cast the first stone at me, if they had been deceived by a false veil of piety. All was finished. And they would never have been able to give enough praise to those who had rendered such great service to the Church: that is what honesty should inspire them to do.

But what seemed perhaps incredible was this: after having publicized the false letter of Father La Combe to all Paris and from there, to the provinces, as a conviction on the errors of Quietism, and at the same time, as a justification for the conduct that they had with respect to me in sending me to the Bastille, there was never a question regarding that letter or the issues with Father La Combe during any of the interrogations that they made me endure. What is also very certain proof that they sought to impose on the public and then even more on Rome was their mixing together the investigation concerning the bishop of Cambrai [Fénelon] with mine, so as to render him more hateful to that Court, and justify the commotion they had for his views, which had nothing to do with mine. I shall keep silent about all of this.

Still more proof that Father La Combe could not have written that letter is that during that conversation, they led me to believe that he considered me a saint. What relationship is there between excessive praise and a letter implicating me in crimes? That letter is not even in his style and it is easy to see an affectation in terms suitable for the effect for which it was composed.

In addition, Father La Combe could not have written such a letter without being the most villainous of men, he who had confessed me for such a long time and who knew the innermost recesses of my heart.[16] But I was so far removed from such a thought, since I had always esteemed him highly and considered him as the one of the greatest servants of God on earth. If God does not permit his innocence to be recognized during his life, then they will see with astonishment, in eternity, the immense weight of glory reserved for him in heaven for his suffering here on earth.[17]

I even found a way to send a copy of this letter to the same person[18] and asked immediately that it be kept for me, for it will always be easy to see the falsehood by means of the copy when compared to the original. And I found out later that this person still has it.

My first reaction was to go place myself in the hands of the Conciergerie and present my complaint to Parliament, since it was a criminal case. But, since I could not extricate myself from this house, without implicating other people in my case, it seemed to me, since I was imprisoned there by a letter of cachet[19] on orders of the king, I would give them a hold on me, if I took that step; they would not fail to make new accusations against me, accusations better founded than the previous ones.[20] I remained therefore at peace, while I waited for what it pleased God to command me, yet mindful of even greater violence to come.

I found out by means of that good peasant girl that the bishop of Cambrai [Fénelon] asked incessantly about the expression on my face and what I said, but God did not allow them to notice even the slightest change in demeanor or the slightest display of chagrin on my face or in my speech. I was well aware that the nuns observed me carefully and even appeared worried, but I behaved normally and treated them with the same respect while I maintained a profound silence. They shrewdly encouraged me to escape in order to avoid that harsh treatment to which I was exposed. But the trap was all too obvious and I was not at all inclined to do such a thing, for it would have given my enemies justification for their actions against me.[21]

Since Desgrez had fallen ill, I remained in this situation for three weeks. Finally, he had recovered after that time and came to tell me that they had vigorously pressed him to come, but the subject of the visit had prevented him from doing so. He added that they accused me of having committed a thousand crimes in that convent. Since that good peasant girl was there at that moment, I asked her, in front of him, what I had done. "*Alas, Madame,*" she answered, "*Only good and no bad.*" I told Desgrez, "*You know what I told you when I came here: they brought me here only to make accusations against me. Now it has been confirmed.*" He told me in a whisper with almost a tear in his eye: "*I pity you.*"[22]

Desgrez had orders not to leave any papers of mine behind. The priest from Saint-Sulpice believed that this was a way to intercept letters, but he found none. One day as I received something that someone sent me that I had asked them to buy for me—some books—some atrocious printed material was found inside. I would not have paid any attention to it if I had not unraveled the package and found in the papers something horrid. I burned all the papers. If Desgrez had given the order on purpose or if it was just by chance, only God knows, but he had the goodness to help me with this incident as with all the rest.

I must discuss the disposition of my heart and all the sacrifices that God had me endure in that convent of Vaugirard. First of all, despite the stormy times, I was there in a state of great tranquility, waiting from one moment to the next for another command of Providence to which I am devoted without reserve.[23] My heart was in a constant state of sacrifice without sacrificing, content to be the victim of Providence.[24]

One day, I was thinking about nothing in particular when I felt compelled to kneel down and even prostrate myself with the certainty that they would remove my maidservants from me as a way of tormenting me more and tormenting them by making them say things against me. I told them this. They cried bitterly and begged me to pray to God that this not happen. Far from asking God for this, I made a sacrifice for it, for I could only wish for God's will.

Another time, I had a premonition that they would withhold communion from me. I had to sacrifice for this and consent to not taking communion since this was the will of God. All of that did actually happen.

After Desgrez had finished rifling through everything, he told me that I had to go to prison alone without my maidservants. I made no resistance to this and gave no sign of despair. My maidservants were driven to despair when they saw themselves about to be taken away from me. I told them that they should not be attached to anything and that God would be everything for them.[25] I left in that fashion after having seen them placed violently in two separate carriages so that they would not know where they were being taken. They have always been separated and what they made them suffer in forcing them to speak against their mistress defies the imagination, without God permitting so many torments to make them betray the truth. One of my maidservants still has continued to suffer for ten years for having spoken out about the story of the poisoned wine before a judge. The other maidservant whose mind was weaker lost it because of all the excessive treatment and length of time for so much suffering, without their being able to extract from her a single word against me, though she often showed signs of madness. They let her go free later and gave her over to her parents. The good treatment that her family has given her and the care that they have taken of her have completely cured her and she lives there now in peace as a servant of God with all her heart.

They then took me to the Bastille alone.[26]

I forgot to say that since I had double tertian fever, I took quinine tonic wine almost constantly. They went to get it at a local tavern. As a result, although at other times I only needed a pint per day for myself, all the wine that was needed because of the quinine tonic, combined with the rest of it, added up to a great deal of wine in no time. They took account of all the wine consumed by me in a memorandum and when it was shown to the archbishop of Paris, it seemed that I was drinking about two pints per day, because they had neglected to say that it was because of the quinine tonic. Consequently, they reproached me for excessive consumption of wine and meat. I still suffered from such severe stomach pains that I could not eat. I answered the archbishop that I was sure that if he observed me eating, he would find instead that I ate too little, not that I ate in excess. He asked if I had fasted during Lent. They told him that I did. He made a disdainful expression on his face on hearing that. It is certain that I was scarcely in any shape to fast at all, for I vomited up almost everything that I ate. Nevertheless, I fasted during Lent despite these inexplicable pains. I often had to get up at night to drink some wine from Alicante, for I felt I was going to die.

After they had taken away the wine, that nun of whom I have spoken came to speak to me about it, along with other sisters of the community of Paris. She wanted me to say something incriminating so that the sisters could make a deposition against me, because the wine incident did not suffice and they had no real evidence against me. But, I answered nothing. The priest from Saint-Sulpice even had the audacity to say in a letter and in his memoirs that I was not content with the best wine in Paris at a hundred écus the cask, so I sent out for wine from a tavern. That wine was so harmful that I took a bottle of it along with me to the Bastille as proof to justify myself and serve as testimony to what had happened at Vaugirard. A servant girl, who was sweeping out a spider web, made the bottle fall and broke it. The odor alone made her fall ill and it took her a long while to recover. She then died shortly afterwards.

I cannot tell in detail about all that they made me suffer in that convent. All I can say is that I would have considered it a delight to go to the Bastille if they had let me go with my maidservants, or at least with one of them, because I believed that I would only have to answer to M. de La Reynie, a man of principles and full of honor, who would not tolerate any surprises. And as I told them to their faces, I do not fear the truth, only allegations and lies.

NOTES

1. The letter from Father La Combe, who was incarcerated in Vincennes at this point, is dated April 27, 1698, a copy of which is included in Fénelon's correspondence (Gondal, *Récits* 115 n1).

2. This surprising visit from an archbishop in liturgical dress reflects Bossuet and the French ambassadors at the Vatican's intensity of effort to obtain a condemnation of Fénelon's *Maxims of the Saints*.

3. The scriptural reference is 2 Timothy 4:3 "For the time is coming when people will not endure sound teaching, but having itching ears they will accumulate for themselves teachers to suit their own likings."

4. Gondal has identified this nephew of the archbishop of Paris who married the niece of Mme de Maintenon (*Récits*, 117 n3).

5. Gondal argues that this comment implicates the priest from Saint-Sulpice in affairs of the court (*Récits* 117 n4).

6. The archbishop of Paris is referring to Matthew 18:18 in which Jesus tells his disciples about their power to influence both life on earth and in heaven.

7. Guyon suspects that Father La Combe was "put to the question," meaning tortured. This is perhaps true since he wrote Apology in which he denies having had any illicit relationship with Guyon, whom he calls the Lady (Gondal *Récits* 118 n5).

8. When married, Guyon had successfully argued over twenty court cases, including one in which she saved her husband's fortune from a lawsuit by King Louis' brother.

9. The Archbishop of Paris is implying the use of torture. During this era, interrogators were allowed to practice what was called the Water Cure. The suspect was forced to drink large quantities of water that caused extreme internal pain. The Bastille was also known for its development of instruments of torture. See Gelfand 66.

10. Guyon mentions the General Hospital in the first Chapter as a possible prison venue for her, a situation that would have placed her in the company of prostitutes. She may again be calling their bluff here.

11. Madame Guyon is referring to Jesus of Nazareth who said, "I am the good shepherd" in John 10: 14. The Archbishop is also known as a shepherd so Guyon is making an indirect statement that she does not consider him her shepherd. That is why he appears embarrassed.

12. The term seduced does not imply sexual activity but a spiritual seduction with credulous or gullible people. See Ulrike Krampl, "When Witches Became False."

13. Guyon may have been suffering from malaria. The Jesuits had brought the medicine quinine back from Peru in the 1600s to help treat those suffering from malaria in Rome and other places in Europe. As such, Guyon shows her understanding of medicine by taking quinine regularly.

14. Guyon and La Combe never met face to face (Gondal *Récits* 123 n8). See also Urbain 71 and La Combe's "Apologie" in which he denounces accusations of his misconduct with Guyon as a series of falsehoods.

15. As a legal technique, Madame Guyon consistently made any information she received public. In 1700 she is vindicated when Bishop Bossuet states that Madame Guyon is innocent.

16. This idea is reminiscent of Teresa of Avila's theology in *Interior Castle* in the Fifth Mansion and other mansions. The Devil may confuse people about the spiritual state of those who are exercising interior devotion.

17. Guyon had many earlier dreams about Father La Combe in which she foresees his spiritual legacy in their effective ministry. One such dream is in her *Autobiography*, Vol. 1, 256-257.

18. Guyon does not reveal here the name of the person she gave La Chétardie's letter to for safekeeping. Tronc identifies this person as the Duke of Chevreuse, Charles-Honoré d'Albert (1656-1712) (927 n70).

19. These sealed letters from the King took away all personal liberty and could be issued for any frivolous reason.

20. Guyon realizes the difficulty of her incarceration. Resistance would be seen as proof of guilt and this would allow for more accusations to come forward (Gondal, *Récits* 126 n11).

21. Guyon continually refuses to run from confrontations with the legal authorities. Before her second arrest, her friends encouraged Guyon to leave France in order to save herself. Guyon also refused that option.

22. Desgrez also investigated the Affair of the Poisons from 1675-1682.

23. Guyon is referring to the vows she took on July 22, 1672. She vowed to "take for my spouse our Lord, the Child" and "to give myself to him for spouse, though unworthy." See *Autobiography*, Vol. 1, 152, 153.

24. In other words, Madame Guyon accepted her sacrifices and found contentment even in the midst of severe hardships.

25. Guyon expresses here the essence of her belief in spiritual annihilation, i.e., God dwells in the heart most strongly when all else is taken away.

26. Madame Guyon's legendary eloquence is seen in this powerful, one sentence paragraph. She understood rhetorical devices, an art written about by St. Augustine.

Chapter Six

In the Bastille: In the Shadow of a Trial

In the summer of 1698, Madame Guyon is transferred to the Bastille to undergo further interrogation sessions by the dreaded lieutenant of police, René d'Argenson. When a keeper of the keys expresses sympathy for her, her jailor Monsieur du Junca threatens him. She is not only subjected to solitary confinement and deprived of her loyal servants, but one of her new maidservants, required to spy on her, is denied medical care so that they can use her death-bed confession against her. Here Madame Guyon discusses Saint Teresa of Avila who was also falsely accused of being involved with the Illuminati. Guyon cautions against false prophets and indicates that she has been writing for some time against those who mislead people in their spiritual life. In March 1699, the papal Brief "Cum alias" condemns the writings of Fénelon. Madame Guyon hopes that she will be released.

Then I was placed in solitary confinement in the Bastille in a bare cell. I arrived there on the eve of the little feast day of God.[1] At first, I had to sit on the floor. Monsieur du Junca lent me a chair and a cot until my furniture arrived.[2] That lasted about four or five days after which I had my furniture. I was alone with an inexplicable feeling of contentment. But that did not last long, for they gave me a maidservant who had social standing but no property. She hoped to make a fortune out of this, as they had promised her, if she could find out something against me. I felt the anguish of being under surveillance, not because I feared it but because I lost happy moments in which I could be alone with my Master Jesus with nothing to distract me from Him, and I see no other happiness similar to what I spend with Him.[3]

Since among my furniture from Vaugirard they brought me many books, such as the Holy Scripture and other good books, they went to tell the Court that they had brought me a cartload of books. They said that they were very bad books and they ordered that an inventory be taken. M. du Junca had them brought to him and had a scribe do the inventory. They were surprised to see that there were only good books in that collection. They found one book of little emblems on divine love.[4] They noted in their report "Emblems of Love." I told M. du Junca: *"Please include the whole title."* He had trouble doing that. They took the report to the archbishop of Paris who saw nothing less than what they had sent to the Court in the first place, so he did not send the report. He was satisfied with the hearsay evidence that indicated I possessed abominable books.

At first, I suffered enormously as much from harsh treatment that they put me through as from the humidity of the place where no one had set a fire for a long time; this caused me to contract a great painful illness. I could not feel relief even in bed. A loss of consciousness seized me that lasted twenty-four hours. They thought I was going to die. I recovered a bit and I told M. du Junca who was there with the keeper of the keys that I begged him to tell the archbishop of Paris that I was innocent of the things they accused me of and that I would protest this by dying. The keeper of the keys, who was a very honest man, said: *"I believe you, poor lady."* I did not speak for a long time after that, but I heard M. du Junca tell him: *"If you speak of this, you will have only me as your executioner."*

As soon as I was able to speak, I asked to be confessed. Father Martineau came for the first time.[5] I did not know him. I confessed with a great deal of pain. When I began my confession, he summoned a doctor who was downstairs. I was surprised to see that he would not finish hearing my confession. He came back with the doctor. He asked him if I were going to die soon. The doctor answered no, unless new setbacks happened. Then Father Martineau told me: *"I am only able to confess you if you are on the point of death."* I told him that if I had more blackouts, I would not be in a state to confess and thus I would die without confession. He had heard most of my confession. He left without wanting to hear the rest and said that they had forbidden him to confess me, and if I died, since this depended neither on him nor on me, I would be at peace. I do not know if these are his exact words but it is his meaning. And the same speeches were repeated to me several times. I was very truly at peace; I had nothing that caused me trouble on that score since I had placed my fate in the hands of God.

I still had that maidservant who spied on my every word and every movement, hoping to make a fortune out of it. One of my own maidservants sent me, through Desgrez, a stitched bonnet that she had made. That woman unraveled it. There was a note there, written in her own blood since she had no ink, and she informed me on a little piece of paper that I found there, that she would always be loyal to me, despite what they were able to do to her. The maidservant spy took the note and gave it to M. du Junca.

As soon as I was able to sit up in a chair, M. d'Argenson came to interrogate me.[6] He had already been briefed about me and had such fury that I had never seen anything like it before. For I must point out that when they saw that M. de La Reynie had rendered justice to me, they gave him another job and then gave his job to M. d'Argenson, who was linked in all respects to those persons who were persecuting me.[7] I resolved to remain silent. Since he saw that in effect I would not answer him, he went into a furious rage and told me that he had orders from the king to make me speak. I thought it best to obey at that point. I answered. I thought at least that despite his prejudice against me, he would write things down as I said them. I had seen such integrity and good faith in M. de La Reynie that I believed others would do the same.

Although I was very weak, they began an interrogation of eight hours straight on what I had done since the age of fifteen until now, whom I had seen and who had served me. These three points were the subject of more than twenty interrogation sessions, each one lasting several hours. I admit that I lacked courage at that point, for God had allowed this without a doubt as a way to make me suffer greatly. For nothing made me suffer as much as those interrogation sessions in which I was sure I was telling the truth but I feared not telling it exactly because of memory lapses. The shrewd twisting of words that they gave to everything, even for the most correct responses, are things that cannot be expressed. They never phrased them in the same terms or meaning. I would only say that after having been interrogated by M. de La Reynie, I had nothing more to say about any of these things. If I had done anything else since Vincennes, they only had to look up the record, but I became aware of that too late. Besides, since we often delude ourselves and do not believe that malice is as great as it is, I convinced myself that they only wanted to be informed about what I did or did not do, just as I had requested at the beginning, and I was sure that information of this nature would make my innocence apparent everywhere. But we were quite far removed from that idea.

There were false letters in which my handwriting was so well forged that I would have had trouble recognizing the forgery myself. If, except for the difference in style, they had not made me write of the places where I had never been and people I had never met, they insisted on verifying the places designated there, so as not to fall into error. I said that I had never dismissed the maidservants that attended me. As regards other servants, it was done according to the circumstances involved. Some footmen had taken up trades and I could not remember the details. It was something like that.

It came to a point in which they wanted to know about the status of my widowhood. I answered with the truth, point by point, regarding my trip to Gex as well as the trip I made with Father La Combe, during which we took an aging religious to accompany us. They did not want to record any of this. They always acted as if it seemed that I was alone with Father La Combe. On a trip that I made from Thonon to Geneva, a trip of only three leagues, there were five or six of us in the group.[8] M. d'Argenson never wanted to note that down as such, so he wrote: "*She was alone with him in Geneva.*" [9] Anything that I said, they dismissed. He showed me an order from the king—a false one or a real one?—that they should show no form of justice to me.

Once on his own initiative, M. d'Argenson added, speaking about something that happened at M. Fouquet's house, that I was not staying there at that time.[10] I told him that I had never stayed there and that he should not note that down. He told me: "*I will interrogate you about this tomorrow and I will write it down.*" Since I had not seen through all his maliciousness, I believed him and signed the paper. The following day, I told him to correct it since I had never stayed at M. Fouquet's house. He refused to change anything.

It must be mentioned that one of the family members of M. Fouquet's wife was there. She had been married to a man who had two wives, which caused a great commotion. He was put in prison. She was injured because of a terrible fall she had and gave birth prematurely, and they pleaded, for they had to deal with a crafty, deceitful man; it was necessary to keep the child for six weeks to nine months. They baptized him in Saint Germain and the child died when the term was up. They got this story from the priest from Saint-Sulpice. Since they took advantage of all these stories and they embellished the reports for Rome and the Court, they made this matter appear to be my fault without my knowing about it. In order to give it more color, they added that I was not staying yet at M. Fouquet's house, so that it appeared that I had stayed there later on, just at the time of childbirth. Several other things happened to me of this nature that showed M. d'Argenson's malice and bad faith.

He then asked me how many times I had seen the bishop of Cambrai [Fénelon]. I told him: "*I never went to his house. He came to see me by order of the bishop of Meaux*"—as was true—"*and never alone.*" When he came to see me on behalf of the bishop of Meaux, it was about some matters regarding St. Cyr.[11] M. d'Argenson wrote down that the bishop of Cambrai came to see me three times and he never included that it was the behest of the bishop of Meaux. He was even angry that I dared to pronounce his name, as if to do so, I profaned him. When it was a question regarding the bishop Cambrai, he became furious. I told him: "*Sir, a judge should not be so partial and should not show such anger against the persons that he is interrogating or against those that he wants to implicate in the interrogation, or show so much devotion to the party of accusers.*" He became all ablaze and then stopped being the lion to become the fox.[12]

Sometimes, [M. d'Argenson] became angry because of the answers I had for him and he said that someone was giving me advice. They searched everywhere to see if that were possible. They built a wire-mesh trellis on top of the fireplace so that, they said, no one could throw in any messages through there. I told him, for it was true that no one was giving me any advice, since I was under surveillance from all sides and my prison tower was very high. He told me: "*Then an angel is dictating a response to you!*" He said this with so much anger and disdain that fair-minded people who might have seen him would have considered him a man incapable of being a judge in an investigation about which he showed so much passion. It was on that basis of prejudice and anger that he distorted all my responses without hearing but very little of what I said.

One day, as he was leaving, the clerk of the court gathered some papers to put them in a bag and said to me in a whisper: "*Poor lady, I am so sorry for you.*" M. d'Argenson saw that I was standing next to the clerk. I spoke about something else in a loud voice. He cast a terrifying look his way and did not stop staring until the clerk left. During that time, the clerk did not dare look at me.

I admit that if I had been able to anticipate the kind of treatment that M. d'Argenson put me through, so different from what M. de La Reynie did, I never would have responded at all. But, the fear of causing blame for others in not responding made me break the silence that I had sworn to keep. I was suffering from such strange oppression caused by a malevolent, cunning judge who had materials in writing prepared against me and who gave my responses a violent twist in an attempt to slide in his venom. I remained with no defense or counsel, observed from all perspectives and mistreated in every manner. They tried to intimidate me in many different ways.

After he had noted that I was not living at that time at M. Fouquet's house, M. du Junca came to speak to me about the priest from Saint-Germain as a man who was his friend and who knew my business well. Since M. Fouquet and his relative had confided in me about all things, I understood why M. d'Argenson had included their affair in my responses, and I saw all the malice there.[13] Then, the governor and M. du Junca scowled at me with severe and terrifying expressions, but all that did not scare me. The best defense is innocence with confidence.

After these interrogation sessions, so long that they lasted almost three months, something they never did for even the worst criminals, they took another two years, apparently to get information elsewhere.[14] They asked that the woman, whom I had attend me, if I did not speak against religion or if I did not commit any crimes. She told them that I was far removed from that and that I was full of sweetness and patience. She said that I prayed to God and read good books and that I consoled her, for she was in a horrible state of despair, the causes for which I will explain later.

She was a woman of social standing but very poor, in charge of three children. She had found a wealthy merchant from Paris who wanted to marry her and who would have given his wealth to her children and to her, for she had nothing of her own. They made her believe that she should attend a woman in a convent and that all she had to do was see who pleased her; it would only take three months and she would be finished with the affair. Nevertheless, they pressed her to come to the Bastille to speak with M. du Junca. When she came there, they made her go up to a room and they locked her in with me. She remained there for a few days without becoming distressed, for she believed that she would leave there soon to put her own affairs in order. But when she saw that they did not want to let her leave or speak to anyone, she became appallingly depressed. She took it all out on me and said whatever her fury inspired her to say to me. I assured her that I had maidservants whom they removed from me by force and who would consider themselves very fortunate if they could spend their life with me in prison. They turned her over to me by force, just as they retained her there against her will. She calmed down a little. They even promised her an immense fortune if she could say something against me.

Although she was a Thiange on her mother's side, and from a very good house on her father's side, a cousin or rather a niece "Brittany style"[15] of Madame the Marshal de La Motte, she had been raised with such little religious education that she was not familiar with the basic principles that even children learn at an early age. She hardly knew God at all. She thought she could do anything she wanted. She was incapable of being touched by any feeling for God. And since what I could say to her to console her at the beginning was suspect because of the bad impression they had given her of me, she thought that a woman could have a marriage of conscience with a man already married. She thought that all they had to do was promise fidelity to one another to be legitimately married, even though the man had another wife. I had all the trouble in the world trying to disabuse her of that idea.

She believed that she was allowed to steal everything from me. She cut my sheets and she grabbed everything I had because I was a prisoner there. Despite my troubles and the serious illness that I had as a result of the torment from M. d'Argenson, I spent every day trying to prevent her from despair. I did not dare appear sad or even withdrawn in front of her. They would have believed that my sadness was proof of my crime, and contemplation would have been seen as another atrocious crime. They observed me then in every aspect. I guarantee that it was not minor torment.

Nevertheless, that woman was sometimes touched by the goodness that I had for her and by my sweetness. But since they brought her in once or twice a week, for several hours, and took her to some place where they plied her with all sorts of promises and told her that I was a hypocrite and a heretic, when she came back from those conversations, from a room below mine, she looked at me with astonishment and horror. When she had been without speaking to them for a few days, she had esteem for me, but despair did not come to an end because of that.

Finally, she fell sick from so much distress. She had a constant violent fever and an inflammation of the chest. At first, she seemed very ill to me. I begged M. du Junca to have her confessed. He refused this. Nevertheless, she needed confession desperately, for I saw the pall of death on her. I took more care of her than a maidservant cares for her mistress, for I was alone with her. I went without undressing or sleeping for seven nights. I had to empty basins frequently. I did everything with all my heart but without strength. I spoke to her about God as much as I could.

One night I found her very ill and I made her perform acts of contrition. With tears in her eyes she promised God she would not relapse into sin if she recovered. She imagined that as soon as I was no longer with her, the Devil entered and sat beside her bed, so she called to me with terrifying dread. I went there with Holy Water. As soon as I appeared, she said: "*He [the Devil] disappeared.*" Since I saw the state she was in, I begged M. du Junca, as the last authority, to have someone confess her. He told me with a hideous look....(*his response is missing in the manuscript*).[16] That night, she took a turn for the worse. I did what I could to encourage her. When morning came, I could not stand it anymore and I went to bed. She called out to me: "*Madame, come quickly.*" I only had time to get out of bed and put on my slippers. She told me: "*My time is up. I am his, it is done, and I am damned.*" I did what I could to console her.

The care that I took with her, what I told her, the harshness of others who denied her confession, and the fact that she was not allowed to see a doctor or a surgeon who could bleed her, all this made her have great esteem for me and she said: "*Since I am damned, I should not be in your room.*" Since I made it clear that she was gravely ill, a surgeon came with M. du Junca. She said: "*Take me away from here. I am damned.*" They thought they had found the magpie in the nest[17] and that she meant to say that they should take her out of my room because I caused her damnation. She was saying just the contrary that, since she was damned, she should not stay in my room.

They had witnesses for what she was saying. They had a doctor come to whom she said the same thing. They believed they could get many things out of her against me. They came to take her away that evening and they had the chaplain of the Bastille follow her. She had requested the priest or the vicar of St. Côme, but they refused to allow him to come. They hoped that the chaplain could get many things against me out of her and that the testimony of a dying person could carry great weight. But, a seizure took hold of her and she spoke well of me to them, refused to confess to the chaplain and kept on asking for her own confessor. Since she had already confided in me the night before regarding some of her sins, I was very troubled to see her die without confessing in the state she was in. But, since they refused to let her see her own confessor, she ended up falling into absolute delirium. Although her illness was an inflammation of the chest, for which they never bleed a foot, the desire they had to extract something from her against me, for they had nothing yet and only wished to do me harm, made them arrange it so that they bled her foot twice, blow after blow. This treatment caused her death without alleviating her seizures.

They wanted to act against me, in one way or another, with what they alleged they had extracted from that woman, although their efforts failed. So, they told Father Martineau, who came to see me from far away with the idea that he would tell me about it: there were strong accusations from that woman against me. This priest, who believed it in good faith and never went beyond the obvious, made me listen to this the first time I saw him. I did not appear shocked to him, since in effect I was not. For, I was not in any state to invent responses; I did not fear the truth, but I did fear their lies. The priest told me that the testimony of a dying person was very strong.

M. d'Argenson came to see me again with an even more severe expression on his face than usual. He told me that the woman disclosed many things against me, leading me to believe that she was alive and in a state to be able to confront me. Since I am too frank, I answered him that she was dead. He replied to me: "*How do you know?*" I told him that I did not doubt it, although no one had told me anything about it. Since he believed that someone had told me something, he used what she could have declared as she was dying, or so he said. I told him that she had left my room with a brain seizure. When he saw that I did not take the bait, he withdrew his questions and sought other ways to interrogate me about this woman and said my answers had to be made in writing. But God did not permit this to happen.

It seemed that God had taken the side of men at that time, for I felt extreme pressure from inside and outside. Everything was against me. I saw all men united to torment me and to catch me off guard: all the skill and subtlety of the mind of people who possess a great deal of this and who are well educated for that, but I, alone and helpless, felt the oppressive hand of God on me,[18] who seemed to abandon me to myself and my own darkness: a complete abandonment from within, without being able to help myself with my own natural spirit in which all vivacity was deadened. For such a long time in effect, I had stopped making use of my own efforts in order to let myself be led to a superior Spirit! And I had worked all my life to submit my spirit to Jesus Christ and my reason to his control. But, in all that time, I could not help myself either with my reason or with any interior support, for I was like those who have never experienced that admirable influence of God's goodness and who do not have a natural spirit. When I prayed, I only received answers about death. The passage in David came to me: *"When they persecuted me, I afflicted my soul with fasting."*[19] I fasted as long as my health allowed with such rigorous fasting and austere penitence but all that seemed to me like burned straw. And one moment in God's hands is a thousand times greater than any amount of help.

They gave me another maidservant who was the goddaughter of M. du Junca. He led her to understand that he would even marry her so that he could get more information from her than from the previous maid. And he gave her the strongest testimony of his passion. Since she was only nineteen years old, he was convinced that there was nothing that she would not do for those by whom she is loved. He believed he had found a sure way to succeed in his designs and bring merit to himself in the eyes of people who persecuted me.[20] I believe that he would have had some consideration for me if he had not had a desire to please them. He did not conceal it from me and told me that, since he owed his fortune to the Messieurs de Noailles,[21] there was nothing that he would not do for them. They had promised him the governorship of the Bastille. They could always dispense with placing M. de St. Mars in that position, but he was going to die and thus he was taking steps backwards in order to jump forward better. I felt in my heart that he would never be governor of the Bastille, and without understanding why, I told him that often older people outlive younger ones. Nevertheless, they still kept on sending new information to Rome regarding what they were doing with me.[22] Provided that they could add some color to the calumny by means of ingenious tricks, it was enough.

On one hand, Father Martineau told me the most outrageous things, including insults, as if I were the worst of all miserable people. But I saw that he was doing violence to himself in this, since he was naturally honest and he was only following the orders they gave him. Two or three days later, after having said to me all the incredible harsh things possible that I received with such sweetness and peacefulness as if he had said the kindest things to me, he then told me that he was not offending me voluntarily but that he was forced to obey. On the other hand, M. du Junca, who knew nothing of this, except that he believed me to be an extravagant heretic and a loathsome person, said all the harshest things imaginable to me. He could not understand such peacefulness and gaiety of mine in the midst of such adversity. He attributed everything to evil because they had prejudiced him against me. They were all in a state of despair because I did not give them any information despite their fits of rage or by any word by which they could count on to torment me again. But although my natural disposition is to respond quickly, God did not permit it.

When the trial in Rome was lost,[23] they were all triumphant about it, and it was then that for several days, they did not stop insulting me, Father Martineau included. I remained always the same. They came to ask me what I thought the bishop of Cambrai [Fénelon] would do after this. I responded: *"He will submit, for he is too honest to do otherwise."* They believed without a doubt that I would say that they had treated him unjustly. Since I had testified with more strength for him than for myself, they thought I would display extreme chagrin and fits of rage. But they saw in that the same evenness as in all the rest. They asked that little lady whom they had placed near me if I were not very sad. She answered no. When they had done all their manipulations, M. du Junca came on behalf of the archbishop of Paris to tell me that for certain reasons they were sometimes forced to do things that they did not want to do; I should write a letter of excuses to the archbishop of Paris and beg him to come to see me, so that I would be released. I thought that he was speaking in good faith and that I would perhaps be released from that moment on, if I just took a few steps. But I was so accustomed to seeing them set traps for me that I did not doubt that this was another one and that they wanted me to sign a condemnation of the bishop of Cambrai [Fénelon]. I responded to this that I had nothing to ask the archbishop of Paris and even less to say to him, and thus it would be quite useless for him to take the trouble to come, for I did not want to leave prison and I found myself at ease in my solitude. They did not speak to me further. I was quite resolute. If they wanted me to sign that condemnation, I told them that it was not up to women to condemn bishops. I would submit to the decision of the Pope, as the bishop of Cambrai had done.

One might believe perhaps that, after so many interrogations, a forged letter of Father La Combe and so much noise made everywhere, they might give me more forged letters and interrogate me further on these matters. I expected it and even desired it. But they did not speak to me further about this. Nevertheless, they let the rumor fly that they had confronted me about Father La Combe. I would have desired this, but how to confront a man who only spoke well of me and never would have written the letters they attributed to him? They did not find any other means to put this in play except to interrogate me on my entire life, where I had been and whom I had seen, who had confessed me and other things of that nature. But they never spoke to me regarding other things during those interrogations. *"Who accompanied you to such and such a place?"* they asked me. I told them that it was Father La Combe with another aged priest and that there were six of us. They only wanted to record that it was Father La Combe and I, and they said that we would have another occasion to speak of this matter. Then they would record what I wanted.

As soon as the matter had been judged in Rome, they stopped interrogating me, but they refused to confess me. They forcefully tried to get me to say that I did not want Father Martineau to confess me. They led me to believe that it was against the intentions of the archbishop of Paris that he would not confess me; if I asked for the chaplain, he would confess me and let me take communion. Father Martineau, on his side, assured me that he was forbidden to confess me. It was incredible to see the promises and threats that they used to force me to accept the chaplain of the Bastille as my confessor, an unknown Provençal man, although they had always said that since the archbishop of Paris had given me Father Martineau, whom I did not know beforehand, he could give him permission to confess me. I did not know who the chaplain of the Bastille was. I had already experienced what desire to have benefits was. It would be easy to make them believe that I had confessed to that man many things that I had never even thought about. I said that a man of a well-known order had honor and the honor of his order to defend, and that I believed him to be incapable of lying. Thus, I would go to him [Father Martineau] and not to others and he could confess me just as well as any other could. Besides, he had no benefit to gain from this. When later on he had been declared confessor to princes, they came to find me and they told me that his work merited some sort of benefit that apparently, I would take away presently. They made it clear to me all the evil they could to do me.

What was surprising is that Father Martineau, on his side, treated me harshly. Nevertheless, I never wanted to leave him and I persevered until the end. If I had been alone in this matter, my God knows well that I would not have taken so many precautions and that I would have done what they wanted. The Devil made every effort and had people of prayer accused falsely so as to discredit them. But when I think what I owed to God and outraged piety, what I owed to my friends and my family (the least of my worries), I never wanted them to be able to say that I had confessed to any falsehood.

I believe that it is not a bad idea to digress slightly. Since the beginning of the world, the Devil has always played the role of the ape of God.[24] He has played the ape throughout the ages. And when Saint Peter performed such great miracles, Simon the magician tried to imitate him and even surpass him. Consequently, Saint Clement of Alexandria revealed that since there were true Gnostics, admirable men, there were also false ones who did abominable things. In the time of Saint Teresa, truly enlightened by God, there arose in Spain miserable illuminati of the Demon and not of God.[25] In this century in which there are simple people truly inwardly focused in prayer, there have arisen miserable creatures under the control of a certain Father Vautier,[26] elsewhere by other means, so that their abominations, being discovered, would discredit the ways of the Lord and have those who opposed them the most become persecuted. I wrote several letters before being put in prison and before they tormented me, which revealed how much I pursued them and alerted people to guard against them. I have living witnesses for that and since I warned everyone on all sides to defy them, I believe this digression is useful.

NOTES

1. The date of Guyon's incarceration in the Bastille is June 4, 1698 (Gondal *Récits* 131 n1).
2. Documents regarding this well-known prison guard at the Bastille M. du Junca appear in Ravaisson's *Archives de la Bastille* [*Archives of the Bastille*] (Gondal *Récits* 131 n2).
3. In one of Guyon's main influences, the 19th century Quaker Hannah Whitall Smith wrote *The Christian's Secret of a Happy Life* using Guyon's ideas on how happiness can be found in any situation.
4. This book is a collection of engravings the text for which was written by Guyon and published under her name, *L'âme amante de son Dieu, preprésenté dans les emblems de Hermannus Hugo sur ses pieus desires et dans ceux dóthon Vaenius sur l'amour divin* (1917) [*The Soul Lover of His God Depicted in the Emblems of Hermannus Hugo on Pious Desire and in Those of Orthon Vaenius on Divine Love*] (Gondal Récits 132 n3).
5. Gondal does not give notes on Father Martineau other than the spelling in the manuscript (*Récits* 133 n4).
6. René de Voyer d'Argenson (1652-1721) was the successor of M. de La Reynie as lieutenant general of police (Gondal, *Récits* 134 n5).
7. The change of administrations between de La Reynie and d'Argenson reflected a shift in police structure and interrogation techniques. This transition had serious ramifications for Guyon. For more detail, see Ulrike Krampl,"When Witches Became False."
8. During this trip, Guyon still had her young daughter Jeanne-Marie with her. She writes about this in her Autobiography, Vol. 1, 257. She left her daughter with the Ursulines at Thonon so she could be educated.
9. The Bishop of Geneva ordered Father La Combe to be the confessor at the Sisters of Charity at which house Guyon lived. During this time, she influenced a nun to end an improper relationship with a man known as the Little Bishop because he influenced the Bishop of Geneva. Shortly after this, the Bishop of Geneva expelled La Combe and Guyon from his diocese. Guyon writes about this in her Autobiography, Vol. 1, 281-297.
10. Guyon's daughter, Jeanne-Marie Guyon de Chesnoy, was married to Louis Nicolas Fouquet, count of Vaux, son of the famous Fouquet, superintendent of finances who was charged with corruption and embezzling (Mallet-Joris 298).
11. Archbishop Fénelon worked closely with Madame de Maintenon on her school at St. Cyr. As such, Guyon met with both of them as they worked to improve the lives of the female students. Fénelon had written a popular book called, *The Education of a Daughter*.
12. Guyon had developed detailed ideas about what constituted a fair court system. She seems to have influenced M. d'Argenson.
13. Madame Guyon was good friends with Fouquet and his family. Nicolas Fouquet had been Louis XIV's Superintendent of Finances. Louis had him

arrested and put into the Bastille. After a trial known for its injustices, Fouquet was sentenced to life-long imprisonment. His incarceration lasted from 1661 until his death in 1680.

14. Gondal notes that Mme Guyon is completely cut off from outside the Bastille while investigations continue against her (*Récits* 139 n7).

15. "Brittany style" means second cousin.

16. This is a note from the copyist, an indication that this manuscript is probably a copy. It is not in Guyon's hand (Gondal *Récits* 142 n11).

17. See E. Cobham Brewer, *Dictionary of Phrases and Fables*, (Philadelphia: Henry Altemus Company, 1898), under the entry for "Pie". A finding something in the magpie's nest means that it is something unlikely to be found. A common phrase in English is "to hit pay dirt."

18. Guyon is referring to scriptures such as Hebrews 10:31 and I Peter 5:6 that describe the hand of God.

In theology, the hand of God is considered to rest upon the chosen but is a difficult burden to bear. I Peter 5:6 reads, "Humble yourselves therefore under the mighty hand of God, that in due time he may exalt you." This fifth chapter from I Peter is crucial for understanding Guyon's theology.

19. The reference is a rewording of Psalm 35:13, "But as for me, when they were sick, I wore sackcloth; I afflicted myself with fasting" (Gondal *Récits* 145 n16).

20. Community and individual concern about reputation confused many of the issues during this long protracted struggle called the Great Conflict. Because of the royal court involvement, many participants attempted to use this situation for financial gain and enhanced social standing.

21. A reference to the family of the archbishop of Paris, Louis Antoine de Noailles.

22. Michael de la Beydore details the intense lobbying efforts of the French ambassadors to the Vatican in his book *The Archbishop and the Lady*, (New York, Pantheon, 1956.)

23. This is a reference to Fénelon's case in Rome as they sought Fénelon's condemnation. A papal brief dated March 12, 1699, "Cum Alias," condemned his defense of mysticism, *Maxims*. (Gondal *Récits* introductory paragraph 131).

24. In this theology, Guyon states that those who imitate or ape interior prayer are the ones persecuting the sincere ones who pray.

25. Alison Weber discusses the difficulties Teresa of Avila (1515-1582) had with the Inquisition (33-35). Gillian Ahlgren notes that the heresy of Illuminism often caused Teresa to become suspect in her practice of mental prayer. The illuminati, however, rejected "confession of sins, fasts, penances or any other pious acts. Their practice of prayer was Quietistic: no amount of thought, not even the contemplations of the Passion of Christ, could help the soul initiate or sustain the union of wills in dejamiento" (Ahlgren 14). Guyon, however, is concerned about confession and penance even in adverse circumstances, as this part of her autobiography reveals.

26. The followers of Father Vautier are often suspected of being behind these campaigns against mysticism (Gondal *Récits* 150 n19).

Chapter Seven

In the Bastille: The Final Battle

Despite the lack of evidence and no legal counsel, Madame Guyon remains in the Bastille for several more years. Another maidservant, a relation of M. du Junca, who promises to marry her if she cooperates, dies after coming in contact with a bottle of contaminated wine brought from Vaugirard. Her interrogator is still M. d'Argenson. She discusses the condemnation of her books by the Clergy Assembly of 1700. However, a priest is brought in to testify against her and he attempts to commit suicide. Her health deteriorates and she narrowly escapes poisoning by an apothecary. There is an addendum to this chapter that gives details on events that happened earlier in the Bastille. She concludes with the circumstances of her release and conflict with her son Armand-Jacques Guyon du Chesnoy who claims she has been released into his custody. He threatens to return her to the Bastille.

To come back to the issues at the Bastille, I had then the goddaughter of M. du Junca attending me, for he had promised to marry her. He believed he could extract from her all that he wanted against me. They had painted such a frightful portrait of me that she trembled at the idea of dealing with me. She was afraid, she told me, that I might strangle her in the middle of the night. He promised her that she would only be with me as long as she found herself at ease there. He assured her nevertheless that I was of a sweet nature and that I would not harm her.

She came dressed in the manner of a coquette, both in her hairdo and in her way of showing her throat.[1] She was very pretty. She had been raised with an acceptable fear of God. I did not speak to her at first about covering up her throat or removing her Fontanges-tower headdress.[2] I let her do as she pleased. No matter how forewarned she had been against me, she no longer held that prejudice after a week. She acquired a staunch friendship for me along with an appropriate confidence in me. She saw that I prayed to God often. Since she had been in a religious house for so long[3] and she knew that they prayed there, she asked me how one should do it. I gave her some passages from the Passion to meditate on. She took such positive advantage of this that on her own, she covered up her throat carefully and did her hairdo modestly. She had such an extreme fear of death that, when she read to me something she skipped the word "death" without reading it and begged me not to speak of it. In the first days, since she had been prejudiced against me, she pulled my hair when she combed it for me and made me turn my head with blows from her fist. But later, although she was extremely quick, if it had been necessary to give blood for me, she would have done it. I believe that the patience God gave me to endure all that she did to me contributed quite a lot to her conversion.

After having been with me for a little while, she tolerated my speaking about death. I saw that she was mortified in everything. When she had agreed to something that suited her well to wear to mass on Sunday, after having arranged it half way, she decided to wear something else more neglectful, and then went ahead with it. I saw her become undone. She admitted to me later that it was for the following reason. As much as she dreaded prison and death, so was she delighted to be with me. She decided to ask God to let her die next to me and never to return to the world. She asked Him this despite the revulsion that was of such an extreme nature that she fell ill. Insofar as she overcame these things in that fashion, she acquired the ability to pray and her prayers became simpler, with a penchant for recollection.[4]

After she had broken a certain bottle of wine that came from Vaugirard,[5] that I have already spoken of, she fell ill and told me one how M. de…[*in the manuscript*] had wanted terrible things from her, but she had resisted him.[6] He was listening at the door. At first, he came in quite dumbfounded. I understood very well that he had heard everything and I was very troubled about it. He showed later that he had so much aversion to her that if she had consented, he would have removed her from my cell immediately. He brought an apothecary with him who was very loyal to him. A man with no religion, he insisted on giving her a bowl, despite my objections, that he said was a purgative[7] that would prevent her from becoming sick. After she drank it, there was no hope for her recovery. Her fever, which was a light tertian fever, became intense, her face changed, and he himself warned me that she would never recover.

To her credit, she asked God to let her die from this illness, despite herself. They insisted on making her leave my cell so that she could have some air. After she opposed them on this, she would not go out unless she could come back to me. They promised her so, knowing full well that she would never return. She told me: "*If I thought I was dying, I would not go out so that I could die next to you.*" They were in despair that their plan to have her come stay with me as part of their designs and interests had failed so abysmally. Her extreme youth had led them to believe that she would submit to so many promises of wealth that they continually put before her eyes; with this she would say all that they wanted her to say against me. But when they saw just the contrary and how much she remained firm in supporting my interests, they only wished to remove her from me. I took care of her for four months, day and night, with all assistance rendered imaginable. Finally, they took her away while she was still in my presence.

They used her confession to inspire bad feelings in her towards me. But what she saw was so contrary to what they told her that she maintained the truth with a courage that was not typical of a person of her age. They told her to be on her guard against my corrupting her and, since she felt the mercy God had given her since she had been with me, she cried bitterly over the stubbornness of those people. She counted on remaining near me as long as I lived, but after she stayed there for three years, in the same room, it was necessary for her to go. She died two weeks later, for she had become a skeleton.

I did not want anyone else near me. I remained alone for a year and a half. I had a fever for a year, without saying anything.

As soon as that girl, of whom I just spoke, died, they came to tell me about it. I believed I should make known God's mercy toward that poor child. God took her away from the world at the age of twenty-one, so that she would not be corrupted by the following events, for since they no longer wanted her to remain in my company, she would have returned to them

To return to what concerns me, M. d'Argenson came back at the end of that episode, after having been away for two years without interrogating me; he had interrogated me previously for such a long time, as I have mentioned.[8]

Above my room, there was a prisoner whom they had placed there. It appeared that this man was guilty, for he paced day and night without ceasing or resting for even a moment, and he ran around like a maniac. On St. Bartholomew's Day, when we were getting dressed to go to mass, we heard him fall and then we heard nothing more. After mass, they brought our dinner in. I told that young lady: *"Go listen at the door, when they bring dinner up there, for I fear that man there may have done harm to himself."* In effect, when they opened the door, they cried out: *"Go get a surgeon and M. du Junca!"* That man was drowning in his own blood. He had stabbed himself in the stomach. They bandaged him up with so much care that he was healed within eight or ten months. They stitched him up and boasted that it was one of the best cures that they had ever done. If he had stabbed himself in the evening, they would have found him dead.

Things like these often happen in places like these and I am not surprised. There is only God's love, the abandonment to His will, faithfulness to a suffering Jesus Christ, together with innocence that allows one to live in peace in such a place, without which the harshness we must endure there without consolation would throw us into despair. In this place they only let you know what can afflict you and you know nothing of what can please you. You only see stern faces that treat you with the worst sort of harshness. You are without defense when they accuse you. They let the outside world hear what they want. In other prisons, you have the benefit of counsel if you are accused. You have lawyers to defend you, judges who, after examining the truth, enlighten one another. But there [in the Bastille],[9] you have no one. You only have one judge who often is both judge and litigant, as happened to me, who interrogates you as he wishes, who writes what he wants from your responses, who dispenses with all the rules of justice, and you have no one afterwards who can set it right. They try to persuade you that you are guilty and make you believe that they have many things against you. And wretched people who do not know what confidence in God is, or the abandonment to His will, and who besides are made to feel guilty, fall into despair.

To come back to M. d'Argenson, he came back after two years, without his look of fury but dressed in sheep's clothing, in order to make me fall more readily into the trap he had set for me.[10] They never were more congenial with me or offered me more favors than he did for me then. Nevertheless, since they had nothing against me, they believed they had found a way to justify all the previous violence done to me thanks to the man who had stabbed himself in the stomach above my room. He was a priest. I never found out why he was there.[11] All that I know was that he said he had seen me at the Ursuline convent in Thonon and that, if they wanted to save his live, he would say what they wanted against me.[12] It was necessary for him to be in a state of compliance. They interrogated him just as they wanted and he signed a statement.

At first, he testified that since I was very ill, Father La Combe brought me the crucifix and that he remained without returning to his house for more than three hours. This could have been true since he said mass for the nuns and confessed them.

It is important to point out that up until now, after such a great multitude of interrogation sessions that they put me through, they had not yet accused me of anything. These interrogations were held only to see what I had said, saw, and done since the age of fifteen, and where I had been. M. de La Reynie had only questioned me about letters, as I have already mentioned. The clergy had only questioned me about my books. But now, the accusations were taking shape. I will tell what I remember about this.

They questioned me about a notebook of writings that belonged to Father La Combe that this priest said he had seen and in which there was this passage: "*O happy sin that has caused us such advantage.*" There were other words that I no longer remember. I said I had no idea about that, but in any event, they referred to some writings on devotion that he had included on what the Church sings: "*O felix culpa*" [O happy sin].[13] M. d'Argenson refused to note my response and said that this phrase meant something else. He simply put down that I did not remember, without writing what the words "*O felix culpa*" meant.

Then, M. d'Argenson told me that the priest accused me of having written many letters to him in which there were things that were not correct. I responded that since I did not recall ever having seen him; I remembered even less having written to him and if he had my letters, then he only had to produce them. I would never renounce my own handwriting. They wrote my response down.

They told me again that this man had testified, for they read the depositions such as they had written them themselves, that I was a thief, an ungodly person, a blasphemer, an immodest person, a person so cruel that I used to say that "I would chop up my daughter like meat for a paté"—those were the terms — "if I thought God wanted me to or if I put it into my head." They did not give specifics for any particular action done that might have related to any of these crimes, but only what I have just mentioned.

That accusation gave me such immeasurable joy in my heart that I cannot express it, for I saw myself as you were, my dear Master Jesus, in the midst of evil doers. I had my way free to make it clear that when they remove the good that I have removed, it is not a way to take the good from someone else. There were no places where I stayed whose churches did not bear the marks of my devotion. I never delivered any sermon in all my life, as everyone knows. As far as cruelty is concerned, never was there a person so far removed from it, for I cannot bear seeing even a chicken killed. (Besides, the archbishop of Paris, with his mocking airs, had told me in Vaugirard that I had never been cruel to men, although it is certain that this is a chapter on which God had given me grace that I did not deserve, as one can see in the account of my *Life*).[14] There was still the matter of my being a deceitful person and a liar. To all that, I responded only another thing: it was necessary to show when and how I had committed these crimes.

Then, he said that he had seen me in another place, at a priest's home playing chess. I told him that I never learned how to play that game. They said that it was at...[15]. They mentioned one place to me instead of another one, because that spot was called by another name. I said that I had not been to that place. I had stopped at another place coming back from Bourbon, but the priest was not there and that was not the place that they were naming.[16]

They said that this priest had come there to see me and that I pretended that I did not know him and received him very poorly. And then they alleged that I had told him things about myself of such surprising confidentiality that if I had had such sentiments, which never happened, I would never have said such things even to my best friends. They alleged that I spoke against the State, against the bishop of Meaux to whom I had a thousand obligations, and against my best friends. The conversation that they alleged took place with him was the subject of several interrogations. I defended myself as much as I was able regarding the things they asked me. I tried to make them see the lack of correspondence [of these allegations] to what I said regarding persons for whom I had an infinite respect at that time and for whom I will have all my life.

My excessive frankness caused me to make an enormous error, for I kept M. d'Argenson in a spot without answering. Since he himself had made the priest testify and he was writing down anything about my responses that he wished, he told me to my face without shame: *"Ah! I am very satisfied with this interrogation. There is no refuge any more or any evasion!"* Finally, I do not know what terms made me understand that I would never recover from them. I had enough evidence of his malicious prejudice against me that allowed him to be able to do everything without saying anything. But, based on what he told me, after so many questions, nevertheless, he had to interrogate me again the following day about this alleged conversation that he said took place.

He had caused me such trouble that only God knows. Although I was resolute because of God's grace in every event, God allowed it in such a way that I suffered a tearing apart of my insides that I cannot express, for the thirty-five or forty days that this interrogation lasted. Except for two or three times when they made me drink a little wine, all that time I went without eating or sleeping and without being able to do anything else. God sustained me in weighing His hand upon me so that I could live without eating.

I then told M. d'Argenson that I was very surprised that a man, who said I had received him so coldly and had pretended not to know him, would then boast that I had told him such strange things in confidence, things that I never even thought about. For I protest in the presence of God that it was such astonishing nonsense on doctrine that after making me read it several times, I found it impossible to understand anything, even less to make any sense out of it. Then I told him simply, and I believed he was writing this down, that there was no semblance of my having disclosed such confidential matters to a man who complained of my lack of civility and coldness. Besides, his deposition stated that he had only spoken to me for one hour when two days would not have been enough to furnish so many things on subjects and matters of the nature that they were, according to what they told me he said. And directing my words to him, I added: *"How, sir, can a conversation one hour long, like the one he spoke of in his deposition, correspond to all that you wish I had said to him, not to mention the quantity of things that you tell me now that you still want to interrogate me about?"*

D'Argenson soon saw his blunder, but he refused to write down what I was saying and assured me that the following day, at the end of his interrogation session, he would include my thoughts in his report. I understood that my thoughts would be even more advantageous to me when they had added eight more hours to that alleged conversation. The clerk told me: *"I have already made the same comment as Madame, but I should not say anything."* There was still a long piece of paper on which to finish up the interrogation begun, but, taking advantage of my simplicity, he pretended he had other matters to attend to, had the interrogation papers signed, picked them up, and did not return the following day as he said he would. I understood my mistake very well and the maliciousness of my judge, but what to do except to suffer what one cannot prevent?

I believe that what contributed to having this last interrogation take place in which they wanted at all costs to make it look like I was a criminal, was that during the Clergy Assembly of the year 1700, presided over by the archbishop of Sens, they declared in condemning my little book, the *Short Method,* and the *Song of Songs* that it had never been a matter of morals in my regard, since I had always shown a great horror for any sort of dissoluteness.[17] So, they could see this in the official report of that Assembly, written and prepared under the eyes of the bishop of Meaux, the most zealous of my persecutors.[18] There was some evidence that this declaration caused them trouble and obliged them to suspect the unfortunate priest, of whom I have not heard anyone speak since that confrontation.

After that last interrogation, my troubles intensified.[19] I only saw hideous faces. They treated me like a criminal. They came to take several letters from my children away from me that they had delivered to me. I burned some of them. They threatened to make me produce them or else. Father Martineau intensified his insults and harsh treatment according to the orders he had received. They rarely summoned me to go to mass, and when they did, it was through the keeper of the keys, or someone else cut from the same cloth. M. du Junca no longer came, which was a consolation for me, for, as I have mentioned, the hand of God was heavier on me from the inside than the hand of men from the outside. It was at that time that they saw that there was no form of justice observed, for they had made a poor wretched priest say all they wanted him to say. I believed that since these things were founded on a lie, they would perhaps let me die. That thought gave me such joy that I began to eat and sleep well. And when I wished for some distraction, I dreamed of the pleasure I would have at seeing myself on the scaffold. I thought that perhaps they would not wish to do me injustice entirely and that they would grant me grace on the scaffold. Then, to prevent that, I would tell the executioner, as soon as I was up there, to do his job. And grace would come after the blow given. I would have pleasure in dying for my dear Master Jesus.

I have some responsibility towards that young lady who attended me, for although she saw that I did not eat and I told her things, she testified always that I was happy and content. It is true that, when I saw someone, God gave me a happy, contented expression. They would have wanted to see me in despair and see me in mortal chagrin, but they did not see anything of that, for although I suffered greatly, I was not chagrined. It was an inner suffering that was consuming me.

Finally, after much time had passed, M. d'Argenson came back. It was no longer a question of this alleged conversation. He did not want to discuss it further. Now new things were being alleged. That priest had said that I lived with Father La Combe in a place where I had been. I made them understand that I lived on the other side of town, in the house of a Treasurer of France, and Father La Combe lived at a young lady's house on the opposite side. The priest said he had seen him at the home of Madame Languet, the widow of the Attorney General. That was true. He said he saw me give Father La Combe some soup. I said that I often gave food to the poor and that I stayed to help him that particular day, but Madame Languet, her daughter and maidservant were also present there and we were putting together a Baby Jesus made of wax. [They said] I wanted to give him some money to go to Rome to solicit a bishopric *in partibus* for the Father, and I promised to give him three thousand pounds per year as a pension to maintain a dignified lifestyle. I said that I was not prepared to promise what I did not have, for I only had an income of two thousand eight hundred pounds and I could only give one thousand écus, especially since I was obliged to pay for my own living expenses and barely had what I needed for that.

Finally, after these childish speeches, M. d'Argenson told me that he would bring that priest to confront me about these matters. He warned that I should not pretend I did not know him. I said that if I knew him, I would say so. He urged me strongly not to become angry with him and I understood that he feared I would intimidate him. After a few days, they brought him in. I must say that they let the rumor spread throughout Paris that they were bringing in Father La Combe to confront me. They never mentioned to me that he had said or written things against me. They only mentioned it to me in passing.

They brought the man to me whom I had trouble recognizing as a man that I had already disapproved of for his disorderly conduct. Without a doubt, this had already been reported to him, but as I say, I still have doubts about it. When I saw him, I told him: *"Sir, why do you accuse me of being a thief, etc.?"* He said he had not said this. I told M. d'Argenson to write down that the priest retracted his statement. I said that I was going to appeal to Parliament and requested the matter be brought there in its current state. I protested the uselessness of all that was done there. I have never seen such a fit of rage as the anger M. d'Argenson displayed. He threatened to go to the king. I answered him that the king would not find it amiss if I defended my innocence before that sovereign Court, for he was too fair a person for that. They then began to read all the depositions against me in the presence of this priest. M. D'Argenson always read from a book without listening to anything, but when he came to the place in the notebook that I spoke of, the priest said: *"Sir, it was 'O felix culpa'[O happy sin] that was said."* Since I kept silent, not wishing to respond after my protestation, I did not gather anything from this, but M. d'Argenson looked at him with anger and said: *"You are a beast,"* for he refused to write the words *O felix culpa* [O happy sin]. When he asked for my response, I kept on protesting the uselessness of this and requested an appeal to Parliament. The priest said nothing at all. Nevertheless, they wrote that he persisted in supporting his declaration. They asked me if I wanted witnesses. I said that I would tell Parliament about the reasons for my challenge and I kept on protesting the groundless nature of the accusations. With this finished, the priest signed the paper, trembling and pale as death. I signed in good faith despite the threats they made to me. I waited a moment for another scene. For M. d'Argenson told me: *"You are tired of being in an honorable prison. If you want to taste the Conciergerie, you will taste it."*[20]

Sometimes, when they were taking me downstairs, they showed me a door and told me that it was there that they tortured. Other times, they showed me a dungeon. I told them I thought it was very pretty and that I would live well there. They said that water came in there. I told them: *"Then, we will place a board up towards the ceiling and put my bed there, my chair, and a ladder for them to bring food to me. I will be just fine there."* They always saw me with the same demeanor despite all the threats. They became tired of making frightful faces at me and left me in peace. M. d'Argenson no longer appeared, although I believed that he could come back at any time.

But the appeal to Parliament hit like a thunderbolt. I fell ill. I was ill for more than a year. I concealed my fever for more than eight months. I was so content being alone that I would not have changed my fate for the queen's. I also saw myself in moments in which I believed I was going to die alone.

One evening, among others, I was alone in my cell and I felt that life was leaving me. I tried to reach my bed to die in it. That cell was a corner that I had made with curtains. I used it as a retreat in one of the transept crossings of my room. But I did not die, for God had reserved other crosses for me to bear. I was delighted to die alone in this way, even though they would not give me confession. I felt an immeasurable pleasure in dying alone with my dear Master Jesus, amidst the abandonment of all things. I would have kept my pain always hidden, if my extreme thinness, coupled with my inability to hold myself up on my legs, had not been discovered.

They summoned a doctor who was a very honest man. He gave me some remedies, but they were useless. The apothecary gave me a poisoned opiate. I found out, after my release, where this poison had come from. I challenged the use of it. I showed the opiate to the doctor who whispered in my ear that I should not take it, for it was indeed poison. The surgeon put his tongue on it and it began to swell up immediately. The apothecary, having gotten wind of this, under the pretext of coming to see me, took the jar from my table and hid it under his cloak. He took it and left.

If in reading this, you pay attention to the crosses that it has pleased God to have me bear, you will also reflect on the care of His Providence to deliver me from so many almost inevitable dangers.

Before the last interrogation, I had two dreams. In the first one, Father La Combe appeared to me attached to a cross as I had dreamed more than twenty years before. But while at that time he appeared entirely brilliant and enlightening, he now appeared pale and covered in bruises with his head wrapped in cloth. He seemed to tell me: *"I am dead."* Yet, he gave me courage. I asked him how he was: *"The sufferings of this life are not worthy to be compared to the glory that has been prepared for us."* And he added forcefully: *"For a light bit of suffering, we have a weight of immense glory."*[21] Then I woke up.

I dreamed later that I found myself walking along a road that imperceptibly led me to a burning coal field with planks covered by earth. I had walked well on top of them. And I saw an even grander field where the flames appeared in some places. This long stretch made me descend. And I found a river below, in such a manner that I did not descend into fire but to enter into the water, and I saw no way out from there. A venerable lady came and gave me her hand and led me to the church of Our Lady. I recalled the passage: "They have passed through fire and water."[22]

*

[Addendum][23]

I was alone for more than a year, for the little lady that I spoke of was dead and I asked them not to give me another one under the pretext that they kept on dying. Thus, I spent my days and often nights without sleep, for I went to bed after midnight and got up later on in the morning. An illness of the eyes befell me in such a fashion that I could not read or work, and although I was quite abandoned within, I was content without the contentment of the will of God.

The trouble I had came from a woman who came to tidy up my room. She had sometimes helped with the duties of Madame de Bernaville,[24] where she had committed theft. She took all that I had from me. She had keys made from mine. Whatever I did, I could not stop her. I did not dare say anything to her, for the chaplain supported her. I said something about this one day to the chaplain who told me that everyone has his vices, and that I had mine, and that this was hers. When she wanted to take one thing from me, I should give her ten with twenty écus to prevent her from taking more. My entire income was not enough for this. I did not doubt that it was a spy that I had on my hands. I had to tolerate these thefts without complaining. On the other hand, they no longer allowed the governor to come see me because he appeared to have consideration for me. They were all surprised at my sweetness and the patience that God gave me, and when I came back from mass to my room, I went up stairs with jubilation.

The governor's nephew told me, when he led me back up, that I was very different from other prisoners who despaired in going back to their cells. I answered him that I found in my cell what I liked and that others perhaps did not. He was not rich. Nevertheless he helped prisoners all he could and had compassion for them. I told him one day that God would surely give him a fortune. He affirmed that he could not have a fortune except at the expense of the life of the governor's son, and he did not wish for it. That son died later and the nephew was the governor's only natural heir. M. du Junca told me, as a way of asking forgiveness for the trouble he caused me, that he owed his fortune to the de Noailles family, for whom his father had been a servant. He said he would be governor of the Bastille after the death of M. de Saint-Mars, who did not have long to live. I told him that young people often die before older ones do. I could not get it out of my head that he would die before the governor. In effect, he did die before him. What good did his desire for fortune do, with such attention to other matters at the expense of charity and justice?[25]

After seven or eight months of illness, I was given the chance to request to see my children. I responded that I had nothing to request. If I had something to ask for, it would be to go to confession. Since they refused to let me confess, I asked for nothing more. They had spoken to my children to make them request to see me. It was not difficult for them to get what they wanted to give them [my children] before they asked for it.[26] My children came. And I lost the sweetness of my life from that moment on because of the torments they caused me. As soon my oldest son arrived,[27] they began quarreling without ceasing in front of me and made me suffer greatly.

I had neither thought nor desire to leave prison. I imagined that I would stay there for the rest of my life. The thought of remaining there alone gave me great pleasure. I felt myself becoming weaker every day and I awaited the end of my life with delight.

The archbishop of Paris had great remorse in leaving me to die in prison, as he admitted openly to his friends. I found this out later from a reliable source.[28] He once said that there was only hearsay evidence against me and he knew of no evil in me.

The priest from Saint-Sulpice tried to strengthen the archbishop's resolve against me and tried to take away his scruples from him, but they were so troublesome that the archbishop could not sleep at night.

[The archbishop] sent word to my children that they should request my freedom and that he would approve the paperwork that they had to do for it. He could not request my release himself for certain reasons. It is easy to understand that a man of his rank and character does not back down easily when they have pushed things to extremes. As far as I am concerned, I came to the conclusion that his reputation was more important to the Church than mine and that he would not be forced to destroy himself because of my case.[29] He could only say that he had been surprised by the appearance of things that they had accused me of, but that after having examined them deeply, and found they were not true, he had to let me go free.

It is certain that they let me go to my son's house without conditions when my release had been granted. When my son arrived, he told me that he would only receive me at his home under certain conditions that he wanted them to give him in writing.[30] The archbishop gave him what he wanted with extreme rigor.[31] That bizarre behavior led me to make a resolution to remain at the Bastille and I said that I would not leave. Monsieur de Saint-Mars who found this procedure loathsome offered me another apartment where I would be pleased to reside. Father Martineau advised me to leave. M. Huguet and others advised the same thing.[32] They told me that since I was still there under their feet, they could accuse me of new things merely on a whim. But what made me make up my mind more than anything else was the belief that my conduct justified me in what followed. My friends would also be justified by the goodness that they showed toward me, for as my dear Master Jesus said in thinking about his disciples: *"I sanctify myself through them."*[33] So, I could say for my friends: I justify myself for their sake. For, when I write this, death appears about to seal my fate at any instant, and I do not aspire to anything more on earth than you, O my Lord. You alone, my only reason, have been the glory of God; they only made prayer a wrong in order to attribute crimes to those who practice it sincerely.

Despite my reluctance at going to live in my son's house, I gave in to the pleas they made.[34] But, even though before my release from the Bastille there were some procedures that made me fear being exposed to his hotheaded, violent character. I admit that I never imagined that I would receive the treatment that I suffered during all the time I remained at my son's house. God who has always led me by the cross allowed me to encounter troubles there of a very particular nature. Nevertheless, I went above and beyond the call of duty in attempting to please both him and his wife: little gifts, friendship, and precautions of all sorts. But nothing was capable of winning them over. You alone know, O my God, the nature of suffering of all sorts that I endured during the course of three or four years that I lived with him. But since You did not wish me to take any steps myself to lead me away from the cross in separating me from them, You allowed them to be the instruments of my retreat and the peace and quiet that I did find, although I never was dependent on their interest.

My presence began to annoy them tremendously for reasons that I shall not mention. They wrote a letter to M. de Pontchartrain,[35] who had the authority to send me back to the Bastille: if he could establish the truth of the allegations that the letter contained, that minister could send the information to the bishop of Blois [Monsignor Bertier].

That prelate was informed not only about the violent character of my son and the poor treatment I endured continually, for he took no care to hide these things, but also about the motives that caused my son to take steps of this nature, which I will reveal with a few examples. The bishop of Blois wrote to the Court regarding my case in a very honest way. He changed the impression that my son's letter had caused there, and then the bishop himself proposed to have me change residence, which was approved. They had him draw up the order himself for this, and he insisted on taking the trouble to come to my son's home to put it into effect. Although my son basically was glad about this separation, the manner in which it was carried out displeased him. He made the bishop of Blois understand that he was in charge of my conduct upon my release from the Bastille. He was then obliged to take me back there [if I misbehaved] or go there himself. And he showed the letter that he said came from M. d'Argenson, who gave him authority over me. Whatever authority M. de Blois could have over him to make him obey the order of which he was the bearer, he refused to carry it out. M. de Blois promised me to write to M. de Pontchartrain again to remove this obstacle that they had not foreseen.

In effect, a few days later, he received a new order for my son to let me go to a house that I had rented in agreement with that prelate, in a small town about half a league from his house, until new orders arrived.[36] M. de Blois kept the sealed letter, about which he made me write that he had communicated with me regarding this matter and that I would respectfully obey all orders. That prelate showed great kindness on my behalf on that occasion and I owe him the peace and quiet that I have enjoyed in this solitude. Nevertheless, since my life is consecrated to the cross, as soon as my spirit began to breathe after such adversity, my body was overcome by all sorts of illnesses. And almost continually I had sicknesses that often brought me to death's door, for the atmosphere was extremely contrary towards me.

I lived there for three years in this manner, but the owner of the house did not wish to renew my rental contract. M. de Blois approved the idea that I would go to live in the town where I am at the moment and where I do not doubt that my dear Master Jesus has kept watch over me and will continue to do so until the end of my days with the harshest and the strongest crosses, although less dazzling, to bear.

NOTES

1. Mme Guyon was accused of showing her throat also, but Father La Combe denied this ("Apologie" 139).
2. Marie Adélaïde de Scorailles de Roussille, Duchesse of Fontanges (1661-1681), mistress of Louis XIV, invented this hairstyle when her hat was swept off her head and she tied her hair up in ribbons (Mitford 81). Nancy Mitford also includes her portrait by François de Troy (79).
3. Gondal interprets this phase "she had been in religion for a long time" to mean that she had been in a religious house (*Récits* 152 n1).
4. Guyon writes in her commentary on *Song of Songs of Solomon*, "Draw me, O divine Lover! And we will run after Thee by recollection which causes us to perceive the divine force by which Thou drawest us towards Thee." James, *The Spiritual Teachings of Madame Guyon*, 153. The spiritual idea of recollection is originally derived from Plato. Fénelon and Guyon were influenced by the same Greek thought as was St. Augustine.
5. The episode of the poisoning of wine is in Chapter 3 of this prison autobiography.
6. Gondal notes that these suspension points appear in the manuscript, probably an allusion to M. du Junca (*Récits* 153 n3).
7. This purgative is a variety of cinnamon from the cassia-bark tree (Gondal *Récits* 153 n4).
8. The marquis d'Argenson is the lieutenant general of police (Mallet-Joris 176).
9. Guyon does not mention the Bastille here, but alludes to it.
10. Guyon refers to the scripture from Matthew 7:15 about false people who are wolves dressed in sheep's clothing.
11. M. du Junca calls him M. Davant from the Franche-Comté (Gondal, *Récits* 156 n5).
12. Guyon writes of having made a retreat at the Ursulines of Tonon in her Autobiography, Vol. 1, 277. During this period of time, she developed her thought about what she calls "happy nothingness" Vol. 1, 276-277.
13. This is a phrase written by Thomas Aquinas (1225-1274) and used annually in the exsultet sung in the Easter Vigil. The meaning is that the sin of Adam and Eve brought about the wonderful redemption in Jesus Christ, "O happy sin that merited such and so great a redeemer!"
14. Guyon discusses some of her relationships with men in part 1 of her Life (Ch. 18) (Gondal *Récits* 158 n8).
15. The place name is illegible (Gondal *Récits* 159 n10). Tronc has "jonchets" or game of jackstraws or pickup-sticks (969 n111).
16. When leaving the first incarceration, Madame Guyon had informed Bossuet that she had need of visiting the waters at Bourbon. *Autobiography*, Vol. 2, 320.
17. Guyon's books were placed on the Catholic Index of Prohibited Books, a list created during the Counter-Reformation to let Catholics know which books

were considered orthodox. Many philosophers were also on this Index, including the works of Immanuel Kant.

18. The date of this Assembly is July 20, 1700 (Gondal *Récits* 162 n12). See also James ed. *Supplement*: "However, the truth of her answers, the purity of her morals, the constancy of her behavior caused the bishops who reunited at Issy in 1700 to acknowledge her innocence. Bossuet led this meeting. However, Madame Guyon remained three more years in jail after the process, where she was sick and suffering" (93).

19. Although Guyon's honesty and confrontation caused an intense, immediate reaction, as the situation progresses, it seems that this confrontation did indeed end the interrogations and might have contributed to her eventual freedom.

20. The Conciergerie was a state-run prison that had one tower in which prisoners were tortured. The Parliament ran this prison and followed state laws.

21. The scriptural reference in this dream is 2 Corinthians 4:17: "For this slight momentary affliction is preparing for us an eternal weight of glory beyond all comparison."

22. Psalms 66:12: "We went through fire and through water" (Gondal *Récits* 168 n15).

23. The narration goes back to events earlier in chapter 7. Guyon often adds remarks about past events in a kind of digression (Gondal *Récits* 168 n16).

24. Perhaps Mme de Bernaville, wife of the commandant of the Bastille. She is only identified in the manuscript as Madame de B (Gondal *Récits* 168 n17).

25. The digression ends here with a scriptural reference: "What does it profit a man to gain the world and lose his soul?" Mark 8:36. Tronc's edition has a Chapter 8 begin here, "La deliverance" [The Deliverance].

26. This affirmation goes against the notion that Guyon's children had taken the initiative to see her. It was another manipulation of her jailers (Gondal *Récits* 170 n18).

27. His name is Armand-Jacques Guyon du Chesnoy (Mallet-Joris 161).

28. The bishop of Blois, Monseignor Bertier, was in direct contact with the archbishop of Paris, M. de Noailles, concerning Guyon (Gondal *Récits* 170 n19).

29. Guyon excuses the archbishop of Pairs whose weaknesses were well known. This matter was of secondary importance to him (Gondal *Récits* 171 n20).

30. Guyon wrote in length about the problems she had with her eldest son. The child had been impacted by their conflicted home and the mother-in-law frequently spoke about Guyon in negative terms to her son.

Hence, the boy developed problems in relating to his mother. As a young child, he had developed small-pox that left his face scarred. Guyon writes, "His face . . . had become like a ploughed field." *Autobiography* vol 1, 122. She details the problems. "The loss I felt most was to see my son revolt against me, whom they inspired with such a scorn for me. I could not see him without dying of grief. When I was in my room with any of my friends, he was sent to listen to what I said; and as the child saw it pleased them, he invented a hundred things to go and tell them. This caused me the most pain with the loss of this child, with whom I had taken extreme trouble. If I surprised him in a lie, which often happened, I dared not reproach him. He told me, 'My grandmother says you have been a greater liar than I.' I answered him, 'It is because I have been so I better know the odiousness of this vice and the difficulty of freeing one's self from it; and it is for this very reason that I will not suffer it in you.' He used to say very offensive things to me, and because he observed the deference I had for his grandmother and his father, when in their absence I wished to reprove him for anything, he reproached me that I wanted to play the mistress because they were not there. They approved all this in the child, so that it strengthened him in his evil dispositions. . . .I had not the strength to chastise him. Similar scenes often happened, and as the child grew bigger, and there was every probability his father would not live, I feared the consequences of so bad an education. I told it to Mother Granger, and she consoled me, and said that, as I could not remedy it, I must suffer it and surrender it to God; that this child would be my cross." (Vol. 1, 136-137) Madame Guyon had attempted to find help for the son from a spiritual director, M. Bertot. She writes, "I told him the need I had of an ecclesiastic to educate my son, and to remove his bad habits and the unfavourable impressions he had been inspired with against me." (Vol. 1, 190. Following this, her son refused to address her as mother (191).

31. Letters of Pontchartrain confirm this information (Gondal *Récits* 171 n21).

32. Denis Huguet, a member of Parlement and Guyon's cousin, was a tutor for her children (Gondal *Récits* 171 n22).

33. John 17:19: "And for their sakes I sanctify myself, so that they also may be sanctified in truth" (Gondal *Récits* 172 n23).

34. When ending her first incarceration, Guyon's daughter and friends picked her up. *Autobiography*, Vol. 1, 320.

35. The count of Pontchartrain was the minister of finance and later of justice (Mallet-Joris 594-96).

36. M. de Pontchartrain's correspondence on these matters is dated July 25, August 12 and September 15, 1706 (Gondal *Récits* 174 n24).

Epilogue

In this concluding chapter, Madame Guyon makes her final theological statement about her profound annihilation. Using her experiences in the Bastille, she emphasizes that in all situations she remained simple and trusting of God, who is the sources of all goodness and holiness. She describes her spiritual state (called a disposition) as that of unchanging because she is united with God and the divine will. She believes that she left behind ephemeral human desires and found the simple and consummated relationship with God for which she had always sought.

If I speak little of my personal dispositions in these final writings, or not at all, it is because my situation has become simple and unchanging.[1] The reason for this state is profound annihilation for which there is nothing interesting to be found. All that I know is that God is infinitely holy, just, good, content and He encompasses in Himself all benefits, and I, all miseries, for I see nothing lower than myself. I acknowledge that God has given me grace capable of saving a world and that perhaps I have repaid him with ingratitude. I say perhaps because nothing continues to exist in me, neither good nor evil. The good is in God. I only have nothing as my share. What can I say about a state that is always the same, without perspective or variation? For dryness, if this is what I am experiencing, is all the same to me as the most satisfying state. Everything is lost in the immensity of God, and I am not able to desire or think.

If they believe some good in me, they are mistaken, and they do wrong to God. All good is in Him and for Him. If I could have one satisfaction, it would be for what He is and what He will always be. If He saves me, it will be a gratuitous thing, for I have neither merit nor dignity.

I am surprised that they have confidence in this nothingness, as I have said. Nevertheless, I respond to what they ask me without being ashamed if I answer well or poorly. If I speak poorly, I am not surprised about this. If I speak well, I do not try to take credit for it. I go without going, without views, without knowing where I go. I neither wish to go or to stop. Will and interests have disappeared. Poverty and nakedness are my share. I have neither confidence nor defiance. In sum, nothing, nothing.[2] For the little that they make me think about myself, I believe I deceive everyone, and I do not know how I deceive them, or what I do to deceive them. There are times when, at the risk of thousands of lives, I would like God to be known and loved. I love the Church. Anything that wounds her wounds me. I fear all that is contrary to her, but I cannot give a name to that fear. It is like a child at the breast who, without seeing monsters, turns away from it. I seek nothing, but expressions and very strong words come to me suddenly. But if I wanted these words to come, they would escape me and if I wanted to repeat them, the same thing would happen. When I have something to say and someone interrupts me, all is lost. Therefore I am like a child from whom they have taken away an apple without her seeing it.[3] She looks for it and does not find it. I am anguished for a moment because they have taken it away from me, but I forget about it just as quickly.

There is nothing greater than God and nothing smaller than I. He is rich. I am poor. I lack nothing and feel no need for anything. Death, life, it is all the same to me.[4] Eternity, time, everything is eternity, everything is God, God is love and love is God and everything in God is for God.

You would just as soon draw light out of darkness than something from this nothingness. It is chaos without confusion. All kinds of things are outside nothingness and nothingness does not acknowledge them. Thoughts only pass on, nothing stops. I am not able to say anything on command. What I have said or written is in the past. I do not remember it. For me, it is like another person. I am unable to desire justification or esteem. If God wishes one thing or another, He will do what He wants. It does not matter to me. May He be glorified in my destruction or in the reestablishment of my reputation. Either one is the same on His scale.

I do not want to deceive you all. Nor do I wish to deceive you. It is up to God to enlighten us and to give us scraps or fondness for this nothingness that does not come from His place. It is an empty lantern. You can put a light in it. If it is a false brilliance that can lead to a downfall, I do not know, for God knows. It is not my business. It is up to you to make the discernment. One only has to extinguish the false light. The flame will never light by itself.

I pray to God to enlighten you all to do only His will, for when you trampled my feet, you would do me justice and I would not be able to find arguments against it.

Here is what I can say of this nothingness that I would like, if I could desire. I wish to forget completely and eternally. If life were not written down, it would run the great risk of never existing. Nevertheless, I would rewrite about my life at the slightest opportunity without knowing why or what I want to say. O my children, open your eyes to the light of truth! Amen.

I must say here that God is holding me in extreme simplicity, uprightness of heart and broad-mindedness, so that I only perceive things on occasions. For without an occasion to change this, I see nothing. If they said something to my advantage, I would be surprised, since I find nothing in myself. If they blame me, I know of nothing else except that I am misery itself, but I do not see what they blame me for. I believe it without seeing it, and everything disappears. If they make me turn back on myself, I know no good. I see all good things in God. I know that He is the beginning of everything and without Him I am nothing more than a beast.

God gives me freedom and lets me speak with people, not according to my dispositions, but according to who they are.[5] He even gives me a natural spirit with those who also have it, and this with such an aura of freedom that they are content. There are certain devout people whose language is but stammering for me. I do not fear the traps they set for me, I take precautions against nothing, and all is well. [My friends] sometimes tell me: *"Be on your guard about what you say to such and such a person."* I then quickly forget about the warning and I cannot be on my guard. Other times they tell me: *"You said such and such a thing and those people can misinterpret it. You are too simple!"* O prudence of the flesh, you find yourself opposed to the simplicity of Jesus Christ. I leave you to your advocates. For me my prudence, my wisdom is Jesus, plain and simple. And if it were necessary to change my conduct to be queen, I would not able to do it. When my simplicity caused me all the troubles in the world, I could not leave simplicity aside.

NOTES

1. The Epilogue corresponds to Chapter XXI in her Autobiography, Vol. 2, 331. Briefly stated, the Epilogue is a shorter version of Chapter XXI. Everything written in the Epilogue is contained in this chapter, yet the order of paragraphs is different. See Gondal (*Récits* 174 n1).

2. Gondal says that Guyon's last words were "rien, rien, rien" [nothing, nothing, nothing] (*Madame Guyon: Un nouveau visage* 19).

3. Guyon uses the masculine singular "un enfant" here.

4. Guyon's idea here is similar to Psalm 73:25, "Whom have I in heaven but you? And having you I desire nothing upon earth."

5. This paragraph is in the *Autobiography*, Vol. 2, 333.

Bibliography

Aalders, W. J. 1914. *Madame Guyon.* Baarn: Hollandia-Drukkeri.
Aegerter, E. 1941. *Madame Guyon, une aventurière mystique,* Hachette: Paris.
Armogathe, Jean-Robert. 1973. *Le Quiétisme.* Paris: PUF.
Ahlgren, Gillian T. 1996. *Teresa of Ávila and the Politics of Sanctity.* Ithaca and London: Cornell University Press.
Bastide, Roger. 1931. *Les problèmes de la vie mystique.* Paris: Colin.
Bataille, Georges. 1954. *L'expérience intérieure.* Paris: Gallimard.
Bedoyere, Michael de la. 1956. *The Archbishop and the Lady.* New York: Pantheon Books.
Beaude, Joseph.1997. *Madame Guyon.* Grenoble: Jérôme Millon.
Bossuet, Jacques Benigne. 1698. *Quakerism a-la-mode, or, A History of Quietiems: Particularly that of the Lord Arch-bishop of Cambray and Madam Guyone...also an account of the management of that controversie (now depending at Rome) betwixt the Arch-bishop's book.* London: J. Harris and A. Bell.
——. *Oeuvres oratoires* 1926. 7 vols. Edited by Abbé J. Lebarq. Paris: Desclée De Brouwer.
Bremond, Henri.1910. *Apologie pour Fénelon,* Paris: Perrin.
——. *Literary History of Religious Thought in France.* 1929-37. 3 Vols. London: S.P.C.K., and New York, Macmillan.
Brezzi, Francesca. 1998. *La passione di pensare: Angela da Foligno, M. Maddalena de' pazzi, Jeanne Guyon.* Roma: Carocci.
Broekhuysen, Arthur. 1991. "The Quietist Movement and Miguel de Molinos," *Journal of Religion and Psychical Research* 14:139-43.
Bruneau-Paine, Marie-Florine. 1983. "La Vie de Madame Guyon: Frigidité et masochisme en tant que dispositifs politiques." *French Forum* 8, no. 2: 101-108.
——. 1982. "Mysticisme et folie ou l'expérience de Jeanne Guyon." *Papers on French Seventeenth Century Literature* 9, no. 16:37-55.
——. "Mysticisme et psychose: L'Autobiographie de Jeanne Guyon." 1981. Dissertation. University of California, Berkeley.
——. 1998. *Women Mystics Confront the Modern World: Marie de l'Incarnation (1599-1672) and Madame Guyon (1648-1717).* New York: State University of New York Press.
Caussade, Jean Pierre de. 1981. *Traité sur l'oraison du Coeur.* Paris: Desclée de Brouwer.
——. 1931. *On Prayer; spiritual instructions on the various states of prayer according to the doctrine of Bossuet, bishop of Meaux.* Translation by Algar Thorold. London: Burns, Oates & Washbourne, Ltd.
——.1961. *Self-Abandonment to Divine Providence.* Translation by Algar Thorold. London: Burns, Oates & Washbourne, Ltd.
Chavannes, Jules. 1865. *Jean-Philippe Dutoit, sa vie, son caractère et ses doctrines.* Lausanne: Georges Bridel.
Cheever, Henry Theodore. c.1885. *Correspondencies of Faith and Views of Madame Guyon: a Comparative Study of the Unitive Power and Place of Faith in the Theology and Church of the Future.* New York: Anson D. F. Randolph & Co.
Cognet, Louis. 1968. *Introduction aux mystiques rhéno-flamands.* Paris: Desclée.
——. 1958. *Le Crépuscle des mystiques, Bossuet Fénelon.* Tournai: Desclée.
——. 1966. *Le Jansénisme.* Paris: Aubier.

Conn, Marie A. 2000. *Noble Daughters. Unheralded Women in Western Civilization. 13th to 18th Centuries*. Westwood, CT: Greenwood Press.
Dupriez, Bernard. 1961. *Fénelon et la Bible. Les origines du mysticisme fénelonien*. Paris: Bloud & Gay.
Egner-Walter, Ute.1989. *Das innere Gebet der Madame Guyon*. Münsterschwarzach: Vier-Türme-erl.
Faguet, E. 1907. "Fénelon et Madame Guyon" *Revue* 71:7.
———. 1919. *Interrogations et procès de Madame Guyon, emprisonnée à Vincennes après son arrestation à Popincourt, Doc H. 1*, 98.
Fénelon, François de Salignac de La Mothe. 1750. *The Archbishop of Cambray's Dissertation on Pure Love. With an Account of the life and Writings of the Lady, for whose Sake the Archbishop was Banished from Court*. London: G. Thomson.
———. 1992. *Correspondence de Fénelon/texte edité par Jean V. Orcibal*. Geneva: Libratrie Droz.
———. 1907. *Fénelon and Mme Guyon; documents nouveaux et inédits*. Paris: Hachette et cie.
———. 2006. *Fénelon: Selected Writings*. Translated by Chad Helms. New York: Paulist Press.
———. 1825. *Lives of the Ancient Philosophers*. London: Knight and Lacey.
———. 1983. *Œuvres*. 2 Vols. Edited by Jacques Le Brun. Paris: Gallimard.
———. 1971. *Oeuvres complétes*. Genève: Slatkine Reprints.
———. 1954. *Oeuvres spirituelles*. Paris: Aubier.
Forthomme, Bernard and Hatem, Jad. 1997, *Madame Guyon: quiétude d'accélération*. Paris: Cariscript.
Francis de Sales. 1686. *Introduction to the Devout Life*. London: Henry Mills for Mat. Turner.
———.1884. *Treatise on the Love of God*. Translation by Rev. Henry Benedict Mackey, O.S. B. London: Burns & Oates, Limited.
Gelfand, Elissa D. 1991. *Imagination in Confinement: Women's Writings from French Prisons*. Ithaca: Cornell University Press.
Goichot, Emile. 1982. *Henri Bremond, historien du sentiment religieux*. Paris: Ophrys.
Gondal, Marie Louise. 1989. "L'Autobiographie de Madame Guyon (1648-1717): La Découverte et l'apport de deux nouveaux manuscrits," *Dix-Septième Siècle* 164, no. 3: 307-23.
Gondal, Marie-Louise. «L'autobiographie de Madame Guyon (1648-1717): La découverte et l'apport de deux nouveaux manuscrits.» *Dix-Septième Siècle* 164, no. 3:307-23.
———. 1990. *La Passion de croire: Mme Guyon. Textes choisies et présentés par Marie-Louise Gondal*. Paris: Nouvelle Cité.
———. 1990. L'expérience mystique de Mme Guyon: questions pour la théologie." In Dore, J. Introduction. *L'expérience de l'esprit. Revue de l'Institue Catholique de Paris* 34: 57-114.
———. 1989. *Madame Guyon: un nouveau visage*. Paris: Beauchesne.
Griselle, Eugene. 1910. "Interrogatoires de Mme Guyon, à Vincennes, let. 26-12-1695." *Documents d'Histoire* 1: 98-120 and 457-468.
Gough, James. 1772. *Life of Michael de Molinos and Progress of Quietism*. In *Life of Lady Guion*, 308-324. Bristol: S. Farley.
———. 1772. "Comparative View of the Lives of St. Teresa and M. Guion." In *Life of Lady Guion*, 237-239. Bristol: S. Farley.

Bibliography

Guitton, G. 1959. *La Père de la Chaise, confesseur de Louis XIV*. Vol. 2. Paris: Beauchesne.

Gusdorf, Georges. 1980. "Conditions and Limits of Autobiography." In *Autobiography: Essays Theoretical and Critical*. Translation and edited by James Olney, 28-48. Princeton, N. J.: Princeton University Press.

Guyon, Jeanne de la Motte. 1897. *Autobiography of Madame Guyon*. Vols. 1 and 2. Translation by Thomas Taylor Allen. London: Kegan Paul, Trench, Trubner &Co.

———. 1915. *The Book of Job*. Beaumont, Texas: The Seedsowers.

———. 1985. *Christ Our Revelation* Auburn, ME: Christian Books Publishing House.

———. 1716. *Discours chrétiens et spirituels sur divers sujets qui regardent la vie intérieure*. 2 Vols. Cologne [Amsterdam]: Jean de la Pierre.

———. 1806. *The Exemplary Life of the Pious Lady Guion*. Bristol: J. Mill.

———. 1816. *A Guide to True Peace, or, A Method of Attaining to Inward and Spiritual Prayer, compiled chiefly from the writings of Fénelon, Lady Guyon, and Molinos*. New York: Samuel Wood & Sons.

———. 1717. *L'âme amante de son Dieu, représentée dans les emblèmes de Hermannus Hugo sur ses «Pieux désirs» et dans ceux d'Othon Vaenius sur l'amour divin*. Cologne[Amsterdam]: Jean de la Pierre.

———. 1790. *La Sainte Bible.* Paris.

———. 1982. *La Vie de Madame Guyon écrite par elle-même*. Edited by Benjamin Sahler. Paris: Dervy-Livres.

———. 2001. *La Vie par elle-même et autres écrits biographiques*. Edited by Dominique Tronc. Étude littéraire Andrée Villard. Paris : Honoré Champion Éditeur.

———. 1720. *Les justifications de Mme J.-M.B. de La Mothe-Guyon, écrites par elle-même, avec un examen de la IX et X conférences de Cassien touchant l'état fixe d'oraison continuelle, par M. De Fénelon*. 3 Vols. Cologne [Amsterdam]: Jean de la Pierre.

———. 1717. *Lettres chrétiennes et spirituelles sur divers sujets qui regardent la vie intérieure ou l'esprit du vrai christianisme*. 4 Vols. Cologne [Amsterdam]: Jean de la Pierre.

———. 1767-1768. *Lettres chrétiennes, nouvelle édition enrichie de la correspondance secrète de M. De Fénelon avec l'auteur*. 5 Vols. Londres [Lyon].

———. 1713. *Le Nouveau Testament de Notre-Seigneur Jésus-Christ avec des explications et réflexions qui regardent la vie intérieure*. 6 Vols. Cologne [Amsterdam]: Jean de la Pierre.

———. 1714-1715. *Les livres de l'Ancien Testament de Notre-Seigneur Jésus-Christ avec des explications et réflexions qui regardent la vie intérieure*. 12 Vols. Cologne [Amsterdam]: Jean de la Pierre.

———. 1978. *Les Opuscules Spirituels*, Hildesheim, New York: Georg Olms.

———. 1825. *The Life and religious experience of the celebrated Lady Guion*. Translation by James Gough. New York: N. Heath.

———. 1685. *Moyen court et très facile pour l'oraison que tous peuvent pratiquer très aisément*. Grenoble: J. Petit.

———. 1872. *Mystical Sense of the Sacred Scriptures; or, the books of the Old and New Testaments, (including the Apocrypha), with explications and reflections regarding the interior life*. Vols. 1 and 2. Genesis-Deuteronomy. Translated by Thomas Watson Duncan. Glasgow, J. Thomson.

———. 1881. *Poems*. Translated by William Cowper, Esq. London: Gall & Inglis.

———. 1722. *Poésies et cantiques spirituels sur divers sujets qui regardent la vie intérieure; ou l'esprit du vrai christianisme*. Cologne [Amsterdam]: Jean De La Pierre.

―. 1992. *Récits de captivité inédit: Autobiographie, quatrième partie.* Edited by Marie-Louise Gondal. Grenoble: Jérôme Millon.
―. 1685. *Règle des associés à l'enfance de Jésus, modèle de perfection pour tous les estats, tirée de la Sainte Ecriture et des Peres.* Lyon: A. Brisson.
―. 1812. *A Short and Easy Method of Prayer.* Baltimore: B. W. Sower.
―. 1789. *A Short and Easy Method of Prayer.* Philadelphia: Francis Bailey.
―. 1879. *The Song of Songs of Solomon, with Explanations and Reflections having Reference to the Interior Life.* New York: A. W. Dennett.
―. 1982. *Spiritual Letters.* Auburn, Me.: Christian Books Publishing House.
―. 1853. *Spiritual Torrents.* Translated by A. E. Ford. Boston: O. Clapp.
―. 1991. *Torrents spirituels: Commentaire au Cantique des Cantiques.* Edited by Claude Morali. Paris: Jérôme Millon.
Guyon, Jeanne et Fénelon. 1982. *La Correspondance secrète.* Edited by Benjamin Sahler. Paris: Dervy-Livres.
Henderson, G. D. 1934. *Mystics of the North East.* Aberdeen: Spalding Club.
―. 1952. *Chevalier Ramsay.* London, New York: Nelson.
Holcombe, William H. 1883. *Aphorisms of the New Life: with Illustrations and Confirmations from the New Testament, Fénelon, Madame Guyon, and Swedenborg.* Philadelphia: E. Claxton and Company.
Hollywood, Amy M. 1995. *The Soul as Virgin Wife: Mechthild of Magdeburg, Marguerite Porète, and Meister Eckhart.* Notre Dame: University of Notre Dame.
Hugo, Hermann and Guyon, Jeanne Marie Bouvier de La Motte Guyon. 1717. *L'âme amante de son Dieu, représentée dans les emblèmes de Hermannus Hugo sur ses pieux désires.* Cologne [Amsterdam]: Jean de la Pierre.
Hurt, John. H. 2002. *Louis XIV and the Parlements: The Assertions of Royal Authority.* Manchester and New York: Manchester University Press.
James, Nancy C. 1998. *The Apophatic Mysticism of Madame Guyon.* Michigan: UMI Dissertation Services.
―. 2011. *The Complete Madame Guyon.* Brewster, Massachusetts: Paraclete Press.
―. 2009. *The Conflict Over the Heresy of "Pure Love" in Seventeenth-Century France: The Tumult Over the Mysticism of Madame Guyon.* Lewiston, New York: Edwin Mellen Press.
―. 2007. *The Pure Love of Madame Guyon. The Great Conflict in Louis XIV's Court.* Maryland: University Press of America.
―. 2007. *The Spiritual Teachings of Madame Guyon, Including Translations into English from Her Writings.* Lewiston, New York: Edwin Mellon Press.
―. 2005. *Standing in the Whirlwind.* Cleveland: The Pilgrim Press, 2005.
James, William. 1961. *Varieties of Religious Experience.* New York: Collier Books.
Johnson, Jan.1998. *Madame Guyon.* Minneapolis: Bethany House Publishers.
Klaits, Joseph. 1986. *Servants of Satan: The Age of the Witch Hunts.* Bloomington: Indiana University Press.
Knox, Ronald Arbuthnott. 1950. *Enthusiasm: A Chapter in the History of Religion.* New York: Oxford University Press.
La Combe, François. 1772, *A Short Letter of Instruction, Shewing the Surest Way to Christian Perfection.* Trans. J. Gough. Bristol: S. Farley, 295-307. In *The Life of Lady Guion.* Bristol: S. Farley.
―. 1910-1911. "Apologie du P. La Combe par lui-même." Edited by Charles Urbain. *Revue Fénelon* 1: 68-87, 139-64.

Bibliography

Laude, Patrick D. 1991. *Approches du quiétisme: deux études suivies du Moyen court et très-facicle pour l'oraison de Madame Guyon.* Paris; Seattle: Papers on French Seventeenth Century Literature.

——. 1990. "Perspectives of Subjectivity and the Ego in Seventeenth-Century French Thought," *Papers on French Seventeenth Century Literature* 17, no. 33: 531-46.

Le Camus, Etienne, Bishop of Grenoble. 1892. *Lettres.* Paris: P. Ingold.

Le Masson, Innocent. 1697. *La vie de Messire Jean a'Arenthon d'Alex, ev et prince de Genève.* Lyon: Comba.

——. 1699. *Éclaircissements sur la vie de Jean d"Arenthon.* Chambéry: Gorrin, 1699.

Loskoutoff, Y. 1987. *La sainte de la fée. Dévotions à l'Enfant Jésus et mode des contes merveilleux à la fin du règne de Louis XIV.* Genève Librarie Droz.

Lubac, Henri de. 1998. *Medieval Exegesis.* Grand Rapids, Michigan: W. B. Eerdmans Publishing Company.

——. 1998. *The Mystery of the Supernatural.* Translated by Rosemary Sheed. New York: Crossroad Press.

——. 1989. *Theological Fragments.* Translated by Rebecca Howell Balinski. San Francisco: Ignatius Press.

Mallet-Joris, Francoise. 1978. *Jeanne Guyon.* Paris: Flammarion.

Masson, Maurice. 1907. *Fénelon et Mme. Guyon; documents nouveaux et in'edits.* Paris: Hachette.

Matter, J. 1866. *Le Mysticisme en France au temps de Fénelon.* Paris: Didier.

Millot, Catherine. 2006. *La vie parfaite: Jeanne Guyon, Simone Weil, Etty Hillesum.* Paris: Gallimard.

Mitford, Nancy. 2004. *The Sun King.* London, New York : Penguin Books.

Molinos, Miguel de. 2010. *The Spiritual Guide.* Edited and translated by Robert P. Baird. New York: Paulist Press.

Mudge, James. 1906. *Fénelon: the mystic.* New York: Eaton and Mains, New York.

Newman, Karen. 1991. *Fashioning Femininity and English Renaissance Drama.* Chicago: Chicago University Press.

Olphe-Galliard, Michel. 1984. *La thèologie mystique en France au XVIIIe siècle: Le pére de Caussade.* Paris: Beauchesne.

Orcibal, Jean. 1972-1999. *Correspondance de Fénelon.* Paris: Klincksieck,

——. 1940. *Fénelon et la Cour romaine.* Paris: Bibliothèque Nationale.

Poiret, Pierre. 1699. *Recueil de divers traités de théologie mystique qui entrent dans la célèbre dispute du quiétisme qui s'agite présentement en France. Avec une préface ou l'on voit beaucoup de particularités de la vie de Mme Guyon,* Cologne [Amsterdam]: Poiret.

Porète, Marguerite. 1993. *The Mirror of Simple Souls.* New York: Paulist Press.

Redern, H. von. 1920. *Die Geschichte einer Seele: Leben, :eiden und Lehren von Jeanne M. B . de la Mothe Guyon.* Schwerin i. Macklb.: Friedrich Bahn.

Riley, Patrick. 2002. "Blaise Pascal, Jeanne Guyon, and the Paradoxes of the *moi haissable*.". *Papers on French seventeenth century literature.* 29, no. 56: 223-243.

Saint-Simon, Duc de. 1967. *Historical Memoirs of the Duc de Saint-Simon.* Vols. 1 and 2. Ed. and Trans. Lucy Norton. New York: McGraw-Hill Book Company.

Schubart, August. 1858. *Frau von Guion, die freundin Fénelons: zur Geschiste der christlichen mystik.* Weimar: Hof-buchdruckerei.

Scupoli, Lorenzo. 1987. *Unseen Warfare: the Spiritual Combat and Path to Paradise of Lorenzo Scupoli.* Crestwood, NY: St. Vladimir's Seminary Press.

Sedgwick, Alexander. 1977. *Jansenism in Seventeenth-Century France: Voices from the Wilderness.* Charlottesville, Virginia: University Press of Virginia

Seillères, E. Baron. 1918. *Mme Guyon et Fénelon, precurseurs de J. J. Rousseau.* Paris: F. Alcan.

Swainson, William Perkes. 1905. *Madame Guyon, the French Quietist.* London: C. W. Daniel.

Tronc, Dominique, ed. 2009. *Les années d'épreuves de Madame Guyon. Emprisonnements et interrogatoires sous le Roi Très Chrétien. Documents biographiques rassemblés et présentés chronologiquement.* Intro. Arlette Lebigre. Paris: Honoré Champion Éditeur.

Tronc, Dominique, ed. 2001. *Jeanne-Marie Guyon. La vie par elle-même et autres écrits biographiques.* Étude littéraire par Andrée Villard. Paris: Honoré Champion Éditeur.

———. 2003. "Une filiation mystique: Chrysostome de Saint-Lo, Jean de Bernieres, Jacques Bertot, Jeanne-Marie Guyon" in *XVIIe siècle.* 55, no. 218: 95-117.

Upham, P. L. 1870. *Letters of Madame Guyon.* New York: W. C. Palmer.

Upham, Thomas C. 1847. *Life and Religious Opinions and Experience of Madame de La Mothe Guyon.* 2 Vols. New York: Harper & Brothers.

Urbain, Charles. See La Combe, François.

Varillon, Francois. 1954. *Fénelon. Oeuvres spirituelles.* Paris: Aubier.

———. 1957. *Fénelon et le pur amour.* Paris: Seuil.

Ward, Patricia A. 2009. *Experimental Theology in America: Madame Guyon, Fénelon, and Their Readers.* Waco, Texas: Baylor University Press.

Weber, Alison. 1990. *Teresa of Avila and the Rhetoric of Femininity.* Princeton, New Jersey: Princeton University Press.

Wesley, John. 1776. *An Extract of the Life of Madam Guion.* London: R. Hawes.

Wieser, Max. 1919. *Deutsche und romanische Religiosität; Fénelon, seine Quellen und seine Wirkungen.* Berlin: Furche.

Index

d'Argenson, M., xxiv, 70-72, 75-76, 80, 86-91
Annihilation, xvii-xx, 18, 68
Anthony, St., 30
D'Aranthon, Jean, x, 43

Barnabite Order, x
Bastille, xv, 65-66, 69-100
Bernaville, Madame de, 92, 96
Bernaville, M. de, 29, 48
Bertier, M. de, Bishop of Blois, 94, 96
Blois, xvi
Bossuet, Jacques Bénigne, xii-xvi, 1-2, 11, 17, 42, 72, 94
Bould, Geoffrey, xxi
Bourgogne, Louis, duc de, xii

Catherine of Genoa, xx
Catherine of Siena, xx
Catholic Index of Prohibited Books
La Chétardie, Joachim Trotti de, 7-12, 20-21, 32-39, 45-54, 55, 59-60, 93
Chevreuse, Charles Honoré d';Albert, Duc de, 68
Clement of Alexandria, 78
La Combe, François, x-xvi, xix, 3, 6, 15, 27, 40, 57-58, 60-63, 67-68, 77, 86, 89, 91
Conciergerie, 42, 63, 90
Court Cenacle, xii
Cowper, William, xx

Davant, M., 95
Delavau, Marie, xx-xxi, 3, 35-36, 64
Desgrez, xiv, 2-3, 14, 19-20, 33, 64-66, 68, 70
Divinization, xix

Enguerrand, Archange, ix, 7, 48
Eugénie, Mother, 40, 43, 44

Fénelon, François, Archbishop of Cambray, xi, xxiv, 13, 23, 28, 33, 48, 55, 63-64, 67, 77, 80
Maxims of the Saints, xv, 32, 80
Fontages, Duchesse of, 83, 85
Fouquet, Gilles M., 2, 14, 72, 80

Fouquet, Louis Nicholas, 80
Francis de Sales, ix, xx, 30

Gautheir, Abbé, xxii
Geneva, x, 71, 80
Godet, Paul, the bishop of Chartres and Saint-Cyr, 18
Goffridy, Louis, 27
Gondal, Marie-Louise, xxii, xxvii, 101
Guyon, Armand-Jacques, ix, 96
Guyon, Madame Jeanne de La Mothe 80
L'âme amante de son Dieu, 80
Early years, ix
Final Years, xvi
Les Justifications, xix, xx
Short and Easy Method of Prayer, x, 44, 88
Song of Songs, xvi, xviii-xx, 29, 55, 88, 95
Spiritual Torrents, x, xviii, 43
Traveling with Father La Combe, x-xi
Guyon, Jeanne-Marie, 29

Harlay de Champvallon, François de, Archbishop of Paris, xii
Holy Spirit, xvi-xix, 43
Huguet, Denis, 97

Innocent XII, Pope, xv
Inquisition, xi, xix
Issy Conferences, xi-xiii, xvi, xvi-xxi

Jane de Chantal, ix, xx, 30
Jansenists, 4, 29
Jean D'Aranthon, Bishop of Geneva, x
Jesuits, 7, 29
Jesus Christ, ix, 1, 24, 67, 68, 87, 94, 100
Junca, Monsieur du, 69-74, 76, 83-84

Lettre de cachet, xi
Louis XIV of France, xii-xv, 14, 15, 30, 44, 56, 59

Maillard, 27, 30, 59
Maintenon, Françoise d'Aubigné, Marquise de, ix-xi, 48, 59, 67
Martineau, Father, 70, 75-78, 80, 89
Mary, xix
Molinos, Miguel de, xxviii
La Mothe, Abbé de, x-xi

Newton, John, xx
Noailles, Cardinal Louis-Antoine de, Archbishop of Paris, xii, 22, 32-33, 38-39, 43, 46, 52, 58-62, 67, 76, 93
Nouvelles Catholiques, xxiii

Paul, Apostle, 49
Pirot, M., 6, 8, 36, 42
Poiret, Pierre, xx
Ponchartrain, M. de, 94, 97
Purgatory, xx
Pure Love, xvi-xvii

Quietism, xv, xxiii, xxviii, 45

Ramsay, André-Michel de, Chevalier, xvi, xx
La Reynie, Gabriel Nicolas de, xiv-xv, 1, 4-6, 14-15, 22, 32, 66, 70-71, 80
Romanticism, xxii

Saint Cyr School, xii
Saint-Mars, M. de, 76, 93
Saint-Simon, Duc de, Louis de Rouvroy, xi, 18
Seneca, 45, 56
Supplement to the Life of Madame Guyon, xiii, xv-xvi, xxii, 96

Teresa of Ávila, xx, xxviii, 42, 68, 78, 81
Thomas à Kempis, xx
Tronson, Louis, Abbé, 7-10, 17, 21

Upham, Thomas Cogswell, xx
Ursuline Sisters, ix

Vatican, 58
Vaugirard, 20-66, 87
Vautier, Father, 78, 82
Versailles, xi, 46

Vincennes, xxi-xxii, 7, 11-12, 20, 32-33, 36, 47, 60, 67
Visitation Convent, xi